# Norman Fischer

## Selected Poems

1980 - 2013

Norman Fischer

# Selected Poems

1980 - 2013

chax 2022

ISBN 978-1-946104-31-1
Library of Congress Control Number: 2021949526

Chax Press
1517 N Wilmot Rd n. 264
Tucson Arizona 85712-4410

Chax Press books are supported in part by individual donors and by sales of the books. Please visit https://chax.org/membership-support/ if you would like to contribute to our mission to make an impact on literature and culture of our time.

MIX
Paper from responsible sources
FSC® C011935
www.fsc.org

RAINFOREST ALLIANCE CERTIFIED

*dedicated to* Kathie Fischer

& Zen priest Sojun Mel Weitsman (1929-2021)

& Poet and Zen priest Philip Whalen (1923-2002)

# Contents

# Like a Walk Through the Park

1980

# My Father

Now that I am an adult I have the distinct recollection that my father each day after work came home and fell asleep on the couch after dinner. His boss was atrocious. Someone always was needed by him to remain until the bitter end, the factory closed and dark, the people gone, the machines quiet, and in the high ceilinged room a tight feeling of total despair prevailed and this person was my father. He oversaw the manufacturing of snowsuits. This person was my father. Bulky snowsuits for children, one piece, in assorted colors, my father's work. He was 33 years old at that time. And he made a birdhouse with a small hole in the front for small birds to enter. My amazement was — my father fashioned a birdhouse out of nothing with a sloping roof. First nothing, then the birdhouse. (Amazement.) That he would do so was certainly beyond the call and skill of fatherhood. It was a gray decade — it seemed whole armies wearing sealskin coats, bearskin earmuffs and thick reindeer boots advanced relentlessly upon us during the months November through March. We lived each day in our large apartment overlooking the street. War was not unknown. My father had a tremendous temper and a great capacity for endurance. What he did not know, which was considerable, he did not consider. But now that I am an adult with my own children who cry too much and are unreasonably demanding I am more in a position to appreciate the discipline necessary not to drink, not to spend too much, not to be cruel. My father lived through years that came hurtling upon themselves in abysmal succession. Once rigid, he became elastic. Once energetic, tired. Once in command, taking a back seat. My father produced snowsuits for children to wear out in the snowy weather. These were sorely needed. Now that I am an adult, with my own children who smile and sigh in the night, and am repeating, inevitably, the life my father led, I can see that. Eventually, in any given place, snow falls.

ooooo

## March 17

Norman since we have so little time
together in the morning
please put down that book

Norman since
there is little time
left put
that book back

∞∞∞

## Tom

The first step is
I realize I am sick I am hopeless to help myself
The second step
is to realize only God can get me out of this
The third step is I turn it over to God
But when I saw that boy
and the blue violas around his chiseled white chin
I ran over the santolina
and dropped a pallet of steer manure

∞∞∞

## Norma

Norma is unhappy with her present life
When she lived with Peter
things were better
in a certain sort of way
Maybe today
Peter feels as she feels
She smokes her cigarette

ooooo

## Tom

It is actually the body of Christ
One is allowed to hold it with only the thumb and index finger
And use those fingers for nothing else
Wearing purple robes — incense swings —
You eat Christ
Only if you are pure
Otherwise you go to hell for making a sacrilege of a sacrament
You kneel there under the vaulted ceiling never knowing
Next to a short Italian man weeping with prayer

ooooo

## To Alice Notley

I knocked at the door expecting another woman you answered
Startled me with your large eyes wispy figure blue jeans attitude
        of benign amusement through crack in the door
Large house hedges grass years later
Cutting the grass the other woman appeared which began our
        long association hearing her fucking in the bed upstairs
        forty-five minutes I was delighted
Now I read your verse of delicate persuasion a splash alive
        forever beautiful jagged faceted piece the mantilla is lace
Darkly moved as such things are I feel it is the order of the day
I am moved today
Your husband self and two sons life
My wife, self, sons

*

She is laughing she is falling isn't the purse everywhere. She
        is falling into the purse.

She is floating she is full she is everywhere. Everywhere.
        It is true.

She is laughing she is bouncing. Her purse is full. The sun is
        everywhere. This is an old saw.

She is laughing. She is everywhere. Isn't that amusing. She is
        bouncing. Wearing her purse. She is full she is falling she
        is laughing she is true.

How about you?

*

Looking down Page toward Van Ness 7 AM
Pool of sunlight on the street

ooooo

## Palm Sunday Sonnet

Gladiola, stately, red
Our task is more than we can bear
To know a fashion's not to see
The dismal stars overhead
Yet bleeding our mind's eyes total beer
Among grapes and hyacinths
The clear day never dawns aright
Till Zeus' statue cleanest washed
Alas not let us never cease
To search for purity, in the sky
Where all clear sight's a fashion red
To bleed our task to what we bear:
The gladiola stately, red
The dismal stars overhead

ooooo

## Easter Sonnet

The Easter lily opens fully
Upon the wicker basket of your heart
At this dark springtime's passions flowering
What crucible anoints a lack?

Pursing, pursuing, the garden steps alight
Brick walls of our longing, our believing
All our melancholy fences, our heart's
Most dirged rock and strap
The essential fragrance of heart's alighting
Upon the last tempted dark
Of your personal night
The Easter lily lends its fragrance
The garden opens to a sigh

ooooo

## April 12/13

later and later
let me be in it
in it not further
let me later be

in further and later
let me be in it
is it not in it
further and later?

let me further be in it
later and later in
is it not in it?
let me be in

let me be in it
later and further

is it not in it
later and later

later and later
in it not further be
let me be in it
let me later be

*

As I write so
she passes before me
what once she was
she was not so later
and is not now
she cannot be so

*

What I was I did not wish to be
what I wished I was not as to
my what was wishing itself not as
as me being accomplished nothing next to

*

*Be* to *wish*! Not. Did I? Was I what?
*To* as *not*. Was I wished? In what?
As not itself wishing was what my
To next nothing accomplished being my "as"

ooooo

## April 15

He came in, closing the door quietly behind him. It was dark in the room — it was night, the blinds were drawn. He felt: there is someone else in the room. He stood with his back to the door, as if he were afraid to commit himself to entering, though he had already done so. There were no sounds in the room to compare with the sound of his heart pounding in his chest. He whirled around. Air rushed to his lungs. He waited a moment. His eyes adjusted to the light. A table-edge appeared. A vase on a table. He was sweating. Flowers in the vase. The clock ticking. He reached for the gun — it was hard and heavy. The drapes rustled. His breath left him. A pair of hands, clasped, on the table.

ooooo

## April 15

Bat Masterson's last words: "No matter what, everyone gets the same amount of ice. Only the rich get it in summer and the poor get it in winter."

# The Devices

1987

## 3

which were not to the notion of multitudinous things
beginning unborn, unwise, unwashed, and unwished for
to take them apart and by visions of beauty replace
the dust bits and those born of moisture or mothers
Requiring pantaloons and baskets of many clothing
as the moon came up it will be cool for babies which are elves
various stones for the fog comes rolling up and rolling out
of the previous valley which for the gods condense
into the various forms of multitudinous perception

ooooo

## 7

turning away from spells to the practicum the purpose the peevish
dour incidence of do not die now
or change your value system not to be bound by legal rule
which actually can be done
self-realization is free from speech discrimination
the footnote claims assertion and refuting the dust jacket
as the name on the spine contains the kernel of great variety of translation
equal to five candles and six boxes
there is reality and it is not pure nor defiled could be seen event of them

ooooo

15

thoughts people hold and move toward
dour incidence of do not die now
nor cancel the good insurance
gives rise to the impression there is nobody present
still we believe the power of personality saves face
as my themes dissolve in snake-oil grim loudness
people who are seriously unique and die
there will seem to be a unity of feeling and a continuity of identity
so though we are untouched by smoke
like the virtue of the all but unspoken

ooooo

23

there is nothing that is born, no entrance to an ample circularity
dangle, then nothing touching, certainly the
Lost in the ooze of sticking to the point
stance or a particular breathing pattern
in whorls she saw there and Jane
whatever when you approach her
steam complexity and she was confused by
Jane breathing in she knows she
A person who is really settled has
gence, what is — looking at her fingertips
and barn swallow nesting in barn roof

ooooo

## 26

Now the physical power of thought
which were notion of multidinous thing
proceed to know the means and conduct which
            characterizes
the creaking of the table when the floor shifts
the fact of the matter is that there is a little bit
of personality in everyone two kinds of view
1) that you are after my job or
2) that I stand to make a lot of money on this
but after all art becomes a business
self-nature is unobtainable

for Alan Davies

ooooo

## 35

of personality is everyone two kinds of view
what we do do and what we intend
gaps time so there is a what to make and alter at
            tremendous expense
closing the death statistics on because of a bee sting
and the bakers have discovered better ways to bake it
on that account there are irritations having to do with
            the delay
it is afterward not a natural thing that before the
            drum some words concur

yes, wish that though, wish all
to be happy means to wake up, walk, wiggle, and go

for Richard Baker

ooooo

38

Margaret are you weeping or grieving or not knowing
why?
Your quiet room betokens independent brief varieties
of simple wisdom
Doing many larger things can't give us a sense of peace
Fills it these hallowed hallways and trees
I don't know how much longer I can keep this up
isn't it marvelous these simple things and how true
the picture of it is
to wake up shut up and sit down
is not a disgrace and involves everyone
and to this magnificent burning moon

for Philip Whalen

ooooo

39

some materials are repeated while others are invented
anew

some peace haunts the system so it won't work right
and I assume it isn't going to work right and so go
    out at night
although I never leave the worms unattended under
    any circumstances
the long tradition of poetry is all about people avoiding
    the grown-up work
of grown-ups making life difficult and fatiguing and
    unassuming
heel-wall will curve around whole hills
the only answer being to destroy the habitat

ooooo

## 47

I do not belong to the school of causation or the school of no causation
Not today if he had invented things that made black and white
over more and if it rings so made as many
clash over it as her throat trembles this time and this question and this answer
of them there are all of them left
all of them left to them one of them
and there are all of them left to him
making fatigue out of less or
the trees are in their autumn beauty
the woodland paths are dry
the world does shine: all the green and sunlight every which way

    for Ron Silliman

ooooo

48

macaronic dialog which at times shatters with bursts
of enthusiasm
chilly mornings for the bare-bottomed ones as time
slips by in greys
but after all art becomes a business
the professional poet, impressed by vicissitudes, is
brained by a cloud
awaken the desire for emancipation the characteristic
feature of insight
turning away from spells to the practicum the purpose
the peevish
If the door is closed don't enter the room.
A metaphor is like a dancer standing on a black spot
But a symbol is a dancer kicking with both feet and
falling down in conclusion

ooooo

57

all acts do draw down
praise or blame

when language is looked at
reality is bliss

in the case of private sensations
on the plane of moral duty

spurting out therefore a picture
of itself the desk

with its shaved head and tea
friendly people in the kitchen

slipping out of her shoes
across the happy room

ooooo

## 61

When language is looked at
            what is looked at
                        is a form of words

This has nothing to do with
            the essence of goodness
                        how a person will be

His speech is not meaningless
            his intention is clear
                        although his action whirls

Thousands will weep and tear
            up paper redefine the ground
                        bereft of such openings

# On Whether or Not to Believe in Your Mind

1987

I don't think any money should be kept in that drawer

The week-end person should have access to that key.

Try to move it to the other desk.

That's often what happens.

The drawer is never open. You should know where the key is. Anybody should. No change and no stamps.

In the way in which we do it. You have to ask permission to use the bathroom. "May I use the bathroom?" Mere cleverness.

What would be the alternative. I think it's 3:30 but actually it's 12:21. There isn't a gathering. Although it does have some of the same function. Some of the same function.

There's a range of ways of hearing the rules. One thing is: the kids are ill-behaved. And another is: there's no use making comparisons.

We've done that in the past. Several years ago, six, seven, eight years ago. Before we depart. It's your birthday and we would like to have a pizza. Rather you would like to have a pizza, we will accompany you.  You would rather pizza, or, prefer pizza. You would prefer pizza.

Get two half gallons. Don't you think we'll lose our membership card if we don't get Hagen Dazs. Who wants to go to the bathroom? Where did everybody go? Out the door. Who wants to go to the bathroom? Elizabeth does. Shake it up and dance all night. Love's a gamble and I'm glad I'm winning. No one would be interested but me. Oh baby. Now we've already finished the pizza.

Stay for the part about the perennial and herbaceous border.

I won't go to Detroit
I will go.

I'd like to.
Yes, I'd like to go to Detroit.

ooooo

So these days pass and the gimmicks multiply,
A benevolent hierarchy taking care of us all
Just as accustomed paths are washed out, fade away all but.
Let's leave one or two.
It's always a question of going outright toward the greatest hunger
And it isn't going to change no matter what the old-timers say.
If only one person understood!
Large, sweet, searching eyes
Worked themselves up to a frenzy hence Plato hexed the rutting Greeks.
You can't blame him for administering balm to a hunk of displaced meat.
Uh oh, my half hour is up.
Incandescent pen, lackluster ink.
Here is my body, no gainsaying that, the bare chipped
Table leg is just another instance of the unvague.
Plato says the slipper exists perfectly at some distance
But my argument amounts to nothing more than a headcold.

ooooo

But are the steps not determined by the illness
The sensations, not the descriptions. And whatever you include
In thinking also in the middle of a train of thought
Say it was a picture (not a sensation, like hot) can't you
        Observe yourself and say "Who is doing this measuring?"
You expected this and that surprised you — what kind
Of a mistake was it? And is our confidence justified?
What would better relay it to us than success? Such as if you say
        "Fire has always burned me," are you
Just rounding things off? It could possibly remain in the air
And not fall, then he will see the light, it will
Dawn on him that "Aha, now I have it!" but will he be able
        To go on after that?
Because, for instance, where else might he get to so suddenly?
A gesture of resignation.
All right then why not suppose that thinking is always in a Language and
        The rules are sometimes in a Syntax
And the expression is tending toward a technique
Of a concept in a tradition.
Then you have to be too, slight, after all it won't do
        To make a false move. And what about memory & expressions like
A smile? Either you
Have this experience or you don't (to quote the law of the Excluded
        Middle

ooooo

## On Thinking

And after you die, what then? Somewhat? Or only more of the same.
Spring has come; Spring is here: what profits these boots, this beauty?
So when a man laughs

His sleeves shake like bamboo leaves in the cold hills' folds —
Not as you'd imagined. Hence thinking takes the form
          Of plans & schemes in which you are central stage
To grand designs of projected events' passage
And their concomitant consequences: yet you worry and that is why
Thought churns, moves, through all those difficult passages
Somebody else's words tick. I want to find my coat since the party's over
          But it is not necessary to fill out a form.
Other times thinking chases itself like old foxes
          Beads of sweat appear on the brow because you can't remember
The color of your baby blanket. But as such can be
Free of thought, or free for thought, either one.
Thought is in & of the body, that is sure
And thought is a tender one more & more
The boat which is pulling away. Thought grows to go out from the body
To stir all buds to make a Spring
As a line of trees first silent locks the world
And then by thought is caused to stir, unwinding,
A strand the morning hurls to frown.

ooooo

## The Knack

One had the knack
To remember the distant stranger
And the trees that came by the by

Flying by the airplane's window
It was love at first sight
Between me and the dark stranger

His foot, his eye, the speed of the airplane
And the air we breathed in the airplane
Unlike that on land: less smoke

Maybe it was less than love, less or more
To confess the strange wall my head hit
More times than I could count it.

All the people on the earth are struggling
With large walls or the knife-edge of laughter
Glancing up occasionally from their leatherwork

Or needlepoint or never — ending suffering
Flying by. The grace of the place they live in
Is not unseen or colorless. It

Moves by the closing of a door once
And forevermore, weight so dense
And loud with a clatter

We would not suspect it did we not know it was so
Having read it in books
Onward so onward the crushing wheel burns

With a clatter as a reminder
And love burns with its grace to struggle
Strictly to have itself out

Clearly and with nothing lost. A day
Dawns and a night slips by
We spend reading or gazing out a window

One by one the lights of the great
City buildings pale in the dawn
The traffic lights pale in the dawn—

How much we feel for our parents when we die
The grace of gazing out a window
At an airplane in the distant sky

ooooo

Experience may not be wholly linguistic
Though I suspect it is. There
May be a part near the rear of the bench
No one has noticed.
Experience is the most common form
Of ideology. I should be sewing a button on my shirt
Not expounding the truth. It's time
For a disclaimer: "You could write a history of the world
Based on salt." Everything has a name
And therein lies a tale.
Experience may not be necessary at all.
It may just get in the way of experience.
Chuang-tzu knew how the fish felt merely by walking near
The pond. Knowing is an inner condition, unique movement.
Imagine everything as moisture, everything as softness.
A baby's cheek or a cat's fur.
Something like that.

As if I lived with something I could touch, touch every way.
As if, pruning the hydrangea, I could actually be in my hand.
It's a terrible thing that no one elicits a response
From the vibrating leaf.

Oak trees angle, bodies bend, twigs snap,
The owl's head slowly turns.

The possibility of total destruction comes from this abstraction,
That our point of view is so foreshortened, misperceiving the
connection
Between bird and sound, word and pain,
Or the faint movement this way to the faint movement that way.
The odor of desire is no longer appropriate
And to look at bodies of water is no longer allowed.
Chances have been lost forever.
Historical time is shrunk.
Even the most acute people have no idea what to do.
Grills protect entrances and layers of cloth dim the faces of images.
The possibilities for evil are beyond calculation.
Speech loses its power to do anything other than sell.
It's as if a sense organ were dropped
From the inventory of human perceptions.

Whatever is a possibility is therefore a necessity.
Things like the sun cease to make the slightest sense.
At one time it seemed emotion could be softened,
Made to act out a theater of reasonable design
Until a person or an object became changed,
But it's no longer the case that the beautiful
Has any meaning other than the hopelessly foolhardy.
If I drape this planet in strands of flowing green fungus
I'd be beset by a feeling I'd failed my own potential
And in fact I have.
Although love is more overwhelming than ever
This grief is so full it doesn't even exist.

ooooo

## On The Toilet

When it snowed I cleared the walkways of drifts so I could get in and out with supplies. A loaded snow shovel is much heavier than you think. And the day might be bright — as it generally was after a storm that might dump a foot or two of snow on us — and I was quite hot working and had to take my coat off. The glare was very bright. All the shape in the trees was apparent, the branches outlined in snow. It was generally very cold. Water in the bucket froze overnight. Looking back on it now, I think I might always have left the bucket empty at night. Why didn't I put it on the stove? The stove was difficult. It choked, backed up smoke, never burned hot enough, was hard to keep going, could never be stoked for the night without going out by morning. That's why it was so cold in the morning. Looking back on it now, I think if I'd cleaned the flue . . . Possibly I should've gotten another stove. Strange . . . But now I remember I didn't have any money. (To be outdoors, the storm blowing snow around, splitting wood, the light leaking out of the day but coming on in concentrated doses in the houses across the pond) or I was sitting by the stove in the evening, very grateful for the warmth, reading a book or thinking, what was I thinking about, was I thinking in words, how many moods did I experience, was there a quality of circularity to the thoughts hovering around one or two main points that perhaps had not altered since childhood . . . Ponderous . . . I got up from my chair and went to the outhouse. While I was gone a bowl fell off a shelf and shattered to the floor: I heard the crash, came back inside with a tremendous feeling that the most significant event of my life had occurred, unfortunately I was on the toilet and had missed it . . .

ooooo

## You Already Know This

There was a young woman, very voluptuous, with swaying auburn hair, who, by contracting herself into an emanation of light, was able to run her presence up and down the bodies of the men who were bathing in the stream. The men noticed only the initial subtle tingle, then the sensation was so comforting it lulled them into a stupor. Floating under the sun, their skin glinted. Gradually their power of expansion, the power that enabled them to blast huge holes into mountainsides and build great concrete structures spanning abysses, condensed into small hard black balls that sank ever so slowly down into the depths of the water where the woman, by alchemy, transformed them into the blasts of white spray the sea makes on windy days when it breaks against rocks.

# Turn Left in Order to Go Right

1987

## The Moralist

My problems don't mean much
But neither is the century perfect
The lawn needs seeding and my hair
Is falling out. Another day to live
Intention's fruit or pour
Want over more disgust so
I must mention the rigorous night?
Take pleasure in the things around us
Fight to make them last in line

ooooo

## I Think the Very Evening

I would rather done anything than to have it happen
Empty out the mind it sticks like a sliding door
But I hardly knew where it was or anything about it
And I stood for a moment — camera-ready — absolutely miserable
The novel should be banned its lessons detached
We shook hands, she and I, and started talking
Some friendly people pokes their heads from around a corner
As fast as possible, then he went back to Elizabeth
I found he was coming toward me too I ducked and the telephone rang
It was Elaine Dodge the hairdresser so I set off
And had not got three yards from the door when
The thought dawned on me that the super was not going to find
The key — only think! — and there I was! — and it began to rain
Slowly, you know, as it does at this hour of morning
The drops barely making it to the ground
But I know more now than I did then

And will not be fooled into thinking any sort of nonsense
Trying to be friendly and polite but white as the gown she had on
There is no limit to my praise of her and her dancing
That we opened our house to the whole family I thought it
Would have been the death of me, the draft somewhere because
We'd used the passageway for dancing despite the fact that
In the novel the passageway is not used but the novel
Was repeated later on in real life or at the very best
Here in the poem and this time breathless couples glided
Back and forth across the passageway their cheeks flushed heels lifted
Although in the novel in fact the dance never
Took place at all but was merely discussed
The confusion comes in because of the tacit assumption that if this
Then that, if here then there, if thus then so, and so forth
And I stood there as if he did not know quite what to do next
He looked at me, I at him, across the pages of the novel
And by that time the woodpile was shrunken to a fraction of its former size
Allowing for the gap between literature and reality
Or even taking into account the gulf between reality and this
Present writing according to calculations too complex to reproduce here
He would have had to manage without the motor in the rain
And said it did not rain, and I must go
And nearly floated there in this rain
So much so that I was obliged to stop where I was and think

# It is Possible to Exist Without Money One Day

I think it is possible to exist without money one day
If the human heart could be silent that long listening
To what the eye suggests the ear intends
It would be hoarse then with shouting at the febrile landscape as if
Hailing it, unable to leave flowers to the wind
Birds to the seasons. It may be possible to exist without
Money one day assuming there were no one to own the land that the
Land lay open under the sun and it was the people who died
While the land endured seasons but did not dissolve
But then insights would not be jealous of each other if
Sports cars were readily available and chance
Operations would be performed on unsuspecting patients no longer
It may be possible to exist without money one day if you
Consult the President who is lying wearily in bed
Ill with a fever caused by insufficient policies based on unexamined
        desires
There is not an ounce of human flesh nor a drop of human
Feeling smeared over and blinded by greed or
Ideology. The car zooms by the brightly lit though unoccupied
Fast food restaurants. New poets will of course replace us as we
Have already replaced ourselves for the career of a poet
Lasts even less time than that of a professional quarterback the
        injuries
Just as inevitable but the pay much less what moves
The words die in time though the words line up clean and
Eager as ever. It may be possible to exist without
Money one day providing you don't mind a loss of
Identity can live like an animal on the simplest of levels breath
And beat of heart and say it's not enough or not say
Anything at all. You could be really honest that way.
The tiger in his eye is fierce but it is too far

Back behind you to be summoned or even feared
You can plant feet firmly aground only below the level of thought
As if that place existed at all possibly
On a day that it was finally evident you could exist without money

ooooo

## Working Title

Their money stood stacked in a single giant column over in a corner near the sliding doors. The soldiers stood motionless despite the buzzing of the many insects. People appeared one by one until the intersection was teeming. The elevator flashed colored lights. He had a ticket and so was privileged. There in the pool of darkness surrounding the Roma baths a man holding a large shapeless package crouched beside a billowy fern in a large pot. The highway unfurled itself under amber skies. Simultaneously a hundred diners wiped the corners of their mouths and belched in an extensive open air restaurant whose tables were covered with red checkered tablecloths. Pedestrians nervously waited at the intersection three or four deep. The chief of police was under fire because the blue ribbon commission had discovered evidence of wrong doing. Window washers received double pay for duty above the twenty-fifth floor. There was a six car pile up on the freeway exit just beyond the new construction site. This package represents the sum of all our desires. Birds hopping among dried leaves blowing on the street at dawn. Couples in drag laughing as they throw popcorn at one another in the darkened hallways. Music blaring from loudspeakers attached to the tops of streetlamps. Silver sports cars with their headlights on slowly snake up the sinuous streets in solemn procession. Tourists keep score on yellow pads. At dawn a line of traffic lights green yellow and red come on all at once stretching down the hill and then up the hill on the other side of the horizon. A woman in a bright yellow hat holding a baby in one arm hails a cab in the street next to the newsstand. A pack of dogs that look defeated and hungry pull apart a beige couch that someone dumped on the sidewalk underneath the railroad overpass. Down along the block at night a rhythm of brightly colored lit up fast food places with no one in them. A snow leopard pacing up and down his cage in the zoo.

In his youth his temperament was fiery and so to correct this he adopted measures. He wore a hair shirt and an iron chain tied tightly around each ankle. But these caused bleeding that stained the streets wherever he walked and spotted the floors in his hut and so he left off these measures. He secretly caused an undergarment to be made for him and in the undergarment he had strips of leather fashioned fixed into which a hundred and fifty brass nails pointed and filed sharp were driven and the points of the nails were always turned toward the flesh. Each nail he understood as a reminder of himself the painful and actual nature of his temperament and he felt the joy of truth in the blaze of each painful point whenever he moved his body. He had the garment made very tight and so arranged as to go round him and fasten in front in order that it might fit closer to his body. And the knowledge that flowed from this increased situation doubled his appreciation of his character and what was necessary to its correction. He slept in this garment winter and summer. Now in summer when it was very hot and he was tired and ill from his journeyings or when he held the office of lecturer he would sometimes as he lay thus in bonds and oppressed with toil and tormented also by noxious insects cry aloud and give way to fretfulness and twist round and round in agony as a worm does when run through with a pointed needle. It often seemed to him as if he were lying on an anthill from the torture caused by these insects which vied with one another. He cried out for death to come and overtake him and blessed and flattered death coaxing her to come but death would not come only further agony which he strove to increase all the more with his fitful turning and bouncing upon his cot. So as to take away the temptation to swat at or crush the insects he devised another method: two leather gloves, and he caused a brazier to fit them all over with sharp pointed brass tacks and he used to put them on at night in order that if he should try while asleep to throw off the hair undergarment or relieve himself from the gnawing of the insects the tacks might then stick into his body. And so it came to pass that he drove the sharp tacks into his breast and tore himself so that his flesh festered. When after many weeks the wounds had healed he could feel a self satisfied feeling creep upon him and so he tore himself again and made fresh wounds. He continued this tormenting exercise for about sixteen years.

The big bus rounded the curve slightly outside its lane and hit the cyclist head on. The car swerved out of control on the slick road hit a guardrail caromed back toward the hillside then bounced over the edge of the cliff into the gully below. A piece of tile crumbled off the edge of the roof and hit a pedestrian eight stories below. The homeless drunken man raised the lead pipe over his head and brought it down with all his might onto the knee of the Assistant City Planning Commissioner. The jackhammer cracked pieces of sidewalk that had been in place since the turn of the century. With a tremendous crash the two hundred year old redwood tree thundered earthward. The white rats in the laboratory screeched when the cancerous injections were applied. Two cars met head on at the intersection with a loud crunching sound because the traffic light malfunctioned. Soundlessly a child plummets from a twenty fifth story window. The pelting rain and accompanying winds knock down a tractor shed. Huge boulders are rushed down stream in the gushing adamant torrent. A building sways and buckles in the earthquake tremor. The rocket with its crew of scientists blazes into white flame seconds after lift off.

The novelist mercilessly used materials gleaned from confidential situations and intimate conversations with close personal friends. The poet raided his heart for fears and wishes which he portrayed in verse with grand gestures and fustian flourishes. The newspaperman was merciless in his search for evidence which he detailed in a series of hard hitting articles that spared no one. The television commentator smiled cynically while listening to the politician explain the necessity for certain very difficult decisions. The philosopher ate an apple while proof reading galleys of his book comparing Heidegger to Spinoza. He looked out the window at the hill covered with brush that swayed in the wind and speculated as to the distinction between remembering and imagining the feel and effect of the wind and being out in it. He found none fundamentally. The poet wanted to hurry the words but couldn't. The linguist analyzed a passage about death and concluded that it possessed no meaning whatever. The minister put the finishing touches to his sermon with an eye to the cheapest possible emotion on the part of his listeners fear and the promise of a final hope. The salesman repeated the same speech for the thousandth time and really meant it. The lovers spoke their feelings as if they had some inkling of what they were talking about. The novelist constructed moral tales commenting on the society in which she lived as if she did not live in it. The typesetter worked on texts whose meaning or import escaped him. The lecturer paused for a sip of water not knowing what she would say next and not at all curious. The proofreader saw words as clusters of letters. The poet prepared himself for composition by emptying his mind entirely of words. He then thrust his desire forward like fists until one by one like bullets words came precise and destructive. He could feel the physical world recede and become an explanation of itself the emotional world dissolve in a verbal excitement whose circumstances by their nature could not be shared. As he rose first slowly and then more rapidly up into the air from his chair his voice became tinnier yet more authoritative and distinct. Finally hovering above the modest duplex house and repeating very long sentences decorated in every way with unusual words and manipulated measures he melted with tenderness of self love until the outlines of his body became indistinct. The reader looked up from her book at a world of augmented meaning.

After these sixteen years his spirit was quenched and he had a vision that such methods were no longer required of him. Out of gratitude he vowed to imitate the sufferings of our Lord as an offering to this purified sense of himself and so he made himself a cross with thirty protruding iron needles and nails. This he bore on his bare back between his shoulders day and night. The first time he lay down on the cross his tender frame was struck with terror at it and he blunted the sharp nails slightly against a stone. But soon repenting of this womanly cowardice he pointed them all again with a file and placed once more the cross upon him. Whenever he sat down or stood up it was as if a hedgehog skin were upon him. If anyone touched him unawares or pushed again his clothes it tore him. He took to bumping up against the walls of his cell pushing the nails in deeper and as he did so recalling whatever sinful deeds he had performed in his life with a view toward blaming himself and portraying himself as a despicable horrid creature that the physical offering of suffering that he made out of gratitude might be accompanied in equal measure with mental torture as well. At this same period he procured an old castaway door and used to lie on it at night without any bedclothes. He thus secured for himself a most miserable bed for hard pea stalks lay in humps under his head the cross with the sharp nails stuck in his back his arms were locked fast in bonds the horsehair garment was round his loins and the door was hard. In winter he suffered much from the frost. He stretched out his feet bare on the stone floor and they froze tearing the skin whenever he lifted them. His feet were full of sores his legs dropsical his knees bloody and seared his loins covered with scars from the horsehair his body wasted his mouth parched with intense thirst and his hands tremulous with weakness. And these torments he bore with a misery whose underlying basis was his great love for his Master our Lord and for himself whom he understood to be a seed for the universe as it now stood and as it would forever be.

ooooo

## The Army

The army is necessary for a time of crisis
Just as shirts are worn in the summer but shed in the fall
The army protects all us citizens
Like bees suck nectar from peach flowers
The army stands foursquare between you and me and you and me
It's because of the army we can keep as clean as we do
We can have our clothes pressed and our sheets trapped
And we ourselves can be trapped by the army or by ourselves who trap the army
The army seems always so unconcerned about our various lovers
In fact we seem to some extent to go back and forth on this question of the army
Which is as necessary to us as breathing or falling off a log
Without the army we would be nothing

ooooo

## A Press as a Death

Romance is it a lot of forcing
So natural to a way of being with you

Elements of madness in Cambodia near the
Border where Thais are forced to murder the

So I want to take your hand at the movies
And the freshness of your gaze revives me
Whole cities up in smoke half a continent
Reviews and then forgets its ancient past

You could hurt me so the door is open
Just an innocent tryst so seriously ajar
That these brown or black peoples' lives seem cheaper
Only because being multiple they gag first

On our detritus left over bits after we've gone
Into the walls piles of sawdust instead of forests
Drank a glass of wine together of a snowy evening
Then made love warmly this side of panes of glass

Next morning we were ashamed of our story
Needing you feeling foolish and washed up
All the strange emotions, picked over corpses
Kids looking at sad plumes of smoke from far off

They wander from village to village visually alive
With needs such as giants could conceptualize
Oh holy life that forces me to be with you
The nearness of you an indigenous pride

We leaf through the pages of the paper for dates
I want you so much your breasts and hair ache
Like the jeep that was blown up the photo
Of us tattered and charred next to the steak

This isn't how I feel to complicate such a decorated piece
Everyone asking me about bundles of meaning
Rising up and shining over some imagined verisimilitude
So your lips are softer when we kiss and sink

Into a bed of mutual obligation we've nurtured
Or fondled into making just but noticeable demands
The camps are overcrowded sanitation poor
And disease ravages those once nearly immune populaces

Our love grows deeper with the passage of years
As if seeds of lifetimes washed up clean together
Together shards of glass or metal engendered
A kind of weather brief as it is deadly but unforgettable

I want to set the record clear here that we don't really know
How to proceed our views are not on solid ground
But our contemplation of the irresponsible impossibility of helpful
        activity
Only causes us deepening anxiety razor-like in its depth and specificity

The policies of the government are hideous and wrong-headed
Trying to protect a cherished idea we torture a subtle torso
Bombing where we think to soothe and cutting
Where we imagine the seam ought to go

Turning the lamp on against the damned darkness
You walk across the room in the moonlight
Yet every moment of your coming my missing you
Or crossing you always in the mail just there

At the long line up of faces photos of the dead
Quietly rendered and lovely though we don't and can't throw stones

We have to judge on very scanty evidence
We have to hope, love, and seek ultimate closure.

ooooo

## In a Fit

for Charles Bernstein

Just as . . . half submerged but undisguised . . .
In a breeze across the bay where the water . . .
To say it just this once this way is . . .
The language won't permit . . . discrepancies
Over which fish in their wisdom and beauty
In the water, their element, and they could not do otherwise
But then to wiggle, no name for it, blind,
In a rage of expression from the first to the last
Unperturbed like a bird singing . . . lucky
Not to be caught out into another element
So far as . . . wishing it . . . it is . . .
Makes it, copies it out, furthermore this way
Chopping the air at it, floundering, flopping
Like it or not a history . . . forebear . . .
Anonymous ways passed on but not written down
Limbering up exercises, capped phrases like glue
People wouldn't say so now . . . yet . . .
If I could relate . . . it changes it, my
Description, not only the way I feel about it,
The experience, the same idea repeated over again
Is not it but not not it either rather is . . .
A wind here promises that . . . it's fortune,
Off the top of the deck, to lure me away, to

Place with my delicate suggestibility, to put me
More and more into my own mind's pre
Conceptions until they go into . . . the
Meaning isn't . . . in the sense of it but . . .
A lack presumed by the large stone there
Perched somehow on the top of a high hill but
Does not fall off even in tremendous winds
That the ordinary is the marvelous that we're not
Dead yet, the poem I didn't want to write,
Distinct definition of who, place names, to be
In relation a chore and yet . . . faster . . .
Whosoever it is . . . a story turns the pages . . .
The same ones here as there yet re-arrange
Into two or three deeply basic attitudes
People scattered around the lawn in random patterns
Each position impossible but no position also impossible
To say these things that you say I say is what
You say to say once more so that what I say
Reflects again what you have said . . . no more . . .
A wonder of it, born of the same concept and pricked
By it into feverish activity, to feel that way
A marker on the path, a true account of it
Sufficient unto the day, at first I was the words
And it lasted . . . all that long . . . till today . . .
These things indeed do have their effects . . .
Dealing with expectation a pre-supposition . . .
The various examined and unexamined ideas . . .
The knife unable to cut itself although many things
Seem to make sense, on the short wave radio,
Taken to be . . . other than . . . alone for it . . .
Into the past, on into it, and again a terminus,

## *from* The Horse or The Picture

The way I hold my fork is not a conscious
Act of mine alone its energy
Like a cut through a skein of cord
Snaps the tree back and snows fall off

Why it's so hard to achieve love
As the sirens sound all over the city
What world grander than this contains potential
Where trees sway under pressure of winds

I don't know what I mean I mean
A box surrounds all my ideas holds
The significance of my phrases constant
Any argument reveals the soft velvet of terms

So I reach back in the dark for my pillow
The sound of that chord associated with lament
As we grow older do the sadnesses increase
Or rather decrease as we close in on our long rest

Only change is at rest doesn't move
From the point of view of the picture
Nothing remains the same teeth cracked
It's like a river rushing by fed from

These snowy peaks above hidden in cloud
An aspect that makes no impression on the mind
Where no social system escapes its jaws
A glittering white point against a blue sky

A barge is pushed past by a tug
While little waves lap the pier

I'm thinking of the various events of my life
Happening over again at an augmented pace

If you look it up the word love has no particular meaning
People blinded by ordinary sight want
Not only the rows line up and the streets
Go round her feet like tiny cute snakes

Tell them I've had a wonderful life
Tell them I've never been so happy
This delicate shimmering world in which
The tiny parts do shine or glow

In the picture we were given at the beginning
The hole where the tab is inserted
Is a gray sky or a blue sky fantastic
Not as if you remained interested in it

She made a nice meal for my relatives
And we dressed and arrived a few minutes late
Lets go shopping for it at a good store
And find the money for it after dinner

It is later and later and still no dinner
The gulls universally facing north screech
We're looking out over the rocks toward the end
Not knowing we're actually in it already

And still not finding the money!
The money is in the picture! You cry
We embrace fervently our scarves flapping
But it's the wrong answer we do not win the prize

Turning the lens around we make time circular
So what if you can name all the animals
Still some shape is set up and falls down
Your hands are left with the same fingers

Clutching air every little boy remembers
Pretending to be a large indomitable man
Loved by an all-encompassing woman
In a closely guarded encampment by the sea

There thunder bellows from the mountain
Bashed against the burnished rocks
So he keeps this forever in his wallet
Just in case the need for it comes up

Soon he needs to peep through the hole in the bag
And seeing another person the opposite of himself
Is seen madly sewing as he kisses her
The mail is picked up at 5 on the dot

So much of what I say I assume
Already beyond it the main part
The whole world as we can describe it
Not anything in particular to be used

ooooo

## Poem for Bach's Three Hundredth Birthday

Walking with you: although I know how to do it I don't think about it as it's being accomplished. There is a rhythm to the movement of the feet and legs, and the arms, the shoulders, swing too. That would be during the first days of spring, the really pleasant ones, when the factory workers first come out of doors to sit in the street. They are thinking this, yet I am writing about something else. The subject matter is completely hidden: it is not to be found either within the words or between them; nor is it underneath the words; nor is it in the mind. So the empty spaces between things move but don't pile up into each other as in a multi-car accident; and so to love and admire a person is necessarily to misunderstand them, to mistake them for yourself, or for that other part of yourself that feels incomplete and is drawn toward a shiny blue object half buried in the sand. The ocean rolls forward. Bits of debris, driftwood, here and there. Small, faintly reminiscent species dumbly berate themselves for their conceptions of an overall pattern that is repeated again and again, always with subtle variations. No two things are ever alike, but no two things are actually different either. Who do you think will die first, you or I? Perhaps (and I think this is really the case) we'll die at exactly the same instant. And nothing will be left over, no remainder, nothing to carry forward onto the next column of figures. But what began before us continues after us, what began before "beginning" continues after "continuing" ceases to echo down the baroque and convoluted passageways of the human ear, or at least can, with a firm certainty, be said to "continue," because we're stuck with "continuing" or even "not continuing" as the only means of speaking. Although we've never been properly introduced you seem to have gotten my name from someone, perhaps overheard it the day you came to pick up the leftover bread. But I don't have yours and it seems very strange to hear you use it, my name, familiarly. I've never even dreamed of your name. It's some sort of hold you have over me, almost a violation. That one would exchange names, surely the civilized thing to do. Yet I might've had some other name too. My parents considered several others, even preferred one or two to the one they finally chose. I've always felt one of those discarded names to be the true name. Yet I answer when called. The wind today is like an anthem, the water's movement essentially abstract, repeating lines of shadow and light, constantly in flux, yet suggesting an overall pattern you almost imagine you've seen before, or could almost describe. Bodies of water have a distinctly calming effect although their activity is unceasing. Most of the earth covered by water, just as most of the mind is covered with insignificant thought until now and again a powerful wave of emotion crests and flings itself forward and we feel temporarily transcendent, assuming we've even noticed, only later do we return to the constant rocking, roiling, really pleasant, almost joyful back and forth movement which seems to partake in no part of any sense of completion, even of partial completion. Now one way, now another, that's all. Things rise and fall arise and decay, modulate endlessly from purity to impurity, yet there is a rudder to our little boat, there is a forward advancement, a course, a plan, or at least not to say there is, not to feel sure there is, not to obey our sense of certainty, would be a grave mistake. Everything human beings stand for assumes conclusions and improvements, and we keep going over and over the text, replacing old parts with new, adjusting an idling screw, breaking off an old nut, sharpening up the teeth of the gears. That way we produce an activity whose hum resonates precisely with a tone we've had in our head since the beginning, and we feel a positive sense of well being that is almost transcendent. There goes the train but now it is coming again. Sometimes it's carrying lots of passengers, sometimes a few, sometimes cargo, sometimes none. Once in a while we make the light, but most of the time we don't. We notice Spring has come again, and when it's here it's nearly unimaginable that there ever was another season. You can remember the snow but it feels more like a movie scene than anything that actually happened. So each season has different colors but in this way is the same. It is not a matter of strong emotion, and what people call "drama" with its attendant pushing and pulling and various senses of suspense and despair isn't it either. Stones on the beach hold your attention. You've half finished before you ever realize you've begun, and by then the thing has its own steam, you just hold on and literally hope for the best. Next other events occur, like a trail of carelessly discarded clothing between here and the bedroom, and you are amazed at all the fortuitous and really in a way insignificant consequences that have resulted from what was no more than an animal urge, like shitting. People tend to gather together in places, whether for reasons of convenience or because they have a common purpose no one knows. But having come, they eventually assume identities, one dependent on another, until all are enmeshed equally in a kind of story line that seems to possess a plot but in the end is just an abstract movement. Different ones assume different roles, villain, good guys, heroes, etc. and sometimes an individual can change roles in a given lifetime. Things begin rather tentatively, but by the fifth or sixth episode the audience is engrossed with the story: whether Sheila will ever locate Brad, who was presumed dead when his small plane crashed in the Andes; or whether Sean will wrest the company from James, his half brother, by devious and probably illegal maneuvering.

At some point we all wake up and ask ourselves: what are we doing here? Who decides? Are our efforts dedicated to a realistic search for the good and the true; or are we just getting lazy, sinking into the inevitably comfortable slide toward death that seems to be what humans are prone to do about middle age, once the kids have gotten a good head of steam on life going. The kids in fact are a great excuse to "settle down!" as they say, and begin doing some serious thinking about what some with all due gravity refer to as "the future." Not that there isn't any future but nine times out of ten that's not what they mean. What they mean is some quite specific definition of the present that does not include too much looking about from right to left too much asking of difficult questions that in the end don't have answers, too much attentiveness to the fact that there do seem to be patterns that are inescapable. The kids' lives do go on in a marvelous way despite all. There's a blind energy there you have to marvel at, how they know exactly what they want (although of course they have no idea how to get it) from the very beginning, and how their little bodies stretch forward toward tomorrow, sensing, or maybe literally even smelling, destiny standing there in an overcoat reading a newspaper at the corner where the express bus stops. They are born with such a dramatic sense of definitiveness. They don't necessarily want to be here but something propels them forward in tremendous struggle they come inch by inch coursed along by some grand movement like the sea in a very clear direction out into the harshness. It's a grand thing to see them then there, completely formed already, each potential movement of life encapsulated in an inchoate flesh, rather the end of life already present in the beginning, this shining moment if you are in the midst of it. Glorious! Like the angels in bloody chorus four and five parts at the tops of their lungs, blood and fluid in a way monstrous actuality of life's basic intentions. Only later do they, in the course of trying to name themselves, trying to live up to or to make hard sense of the words they are given to know, join the human race with semantron and semaphore, until bit by bit this elemental quality leaves them, or rather doesn't really leave them so much as get defined out; still there but unnoticed. And the word "elemental" isn't it either, but rather points us in exactly the wrong direction. All the words, in fact, are the wrong ones: magical, and all we've got, but essentially wrong, because they point to something, when really there isn't anything. They're like a screen (I almost wrote "scream"), one of those lovely Chinese or Japanese screens behind which the courtesan stands as she speaks to her lover who has never seen her but who is tortured night and day by the memory of the sound of her voice. For instance, simple things, ordinary things, depend on how you view them. Cleaning a toilet is a terrible job if it defines a social class or is seen as dead time, time in which some piece more lofty could be performed. But if you call it a divine act, if you view it as august, improving, and difficult of achievement, it just could be a vehicle for the deepest of self-realizations leading you out of the narrow confines of self-identity and into a wider embracing of the whole of life. There's a kite stuck in the tree outside. And that's our situation. Not to place things of the utmost importance at a distance from us, but to bring God to the human level in all we do or say, that joy there here. And on the other hand not to denigrate obfuscate or berate ourselves too much for what we are but to see the human, all its laziness foolishness baseness and consanguinity, its velleities and its volitions, as God-like in its beauty value and melody, just here in the products of eye and ear, our ordinary visions and chorales. Someone once asked a great painter what was the point of all her works and she answered, think of all the stages I've passed through!

(for Billy Joe Atkinson, who requested that I
write a poem in contrapuntal form for Bach's
300th birthday celebration, March, 1985)

ooooo

## Homage to Philip Whalen

At home the vegetable supply
Along the trailing edge
Of life is the only fit subject
Broad-rim soup dish BLASH
Out there the garbage needs to
BLASH Daitokuji monastery
Churchbells ring over every hand and face
Here at the edge of town people visit me

We've got to have amusement
Let's go in; let's go in deeper
Work, every day, no time to feel sad and friendless
Or have we proven that. We take
(Rapeseed oil waterproof paper umbrella)
We really deserve progression not indigestion
The plum tree functions gorgeously
Let's not go forward at all

ooooo

## Not to be Found

The arbitrary mindless
Persistence of objects ready to
Explode so crowded into themselves
They wait vainly for their masks
To coincide with an earnestness
Folded into prescience
Not to be found in words

ooooo

## Prayer

God grant that I be healthy
Live a long life with family and friends
Under trees in places beauty grows in
But if not that also I wait for the end
I get as if it would by my plunging in

Quiet storms far away bruising others too
And my own destructive deeds assuage
That my sadness in not appearing here again
Be counterbalanced in equal doses of another's joy
And that my saying so be assigned any meaning
It might humbly though momentarily adhere to

ooooo

## To My Mother Lenora Fischer (1923 -1985)

Like no other time before now nor afterward
What I feel for you dissolves my limbs
As if the edges of my body were a lie I was caught in
Or an excuse that only a lie could resolve
I want to break out of this to get to your side
Because the totality of the peace you bring
Puts this world with its trees rumors and meals to shame
And although we never understood each other in ordinary ways
We cannot choose either more or less what we'll be influenced by
The moon is bright tonight just rising over the top of the peak
What tracks will the moon's path leave what marks in the sky?
I will go there. I will embark on this story.
What would it mean
Once it tore itself from me against my will
And who would claim credit?
Would a future life be assured or is the sky
Enough this summer's night whose problem
Does not seem a problem from your side
Time's slide greased by thought our love
Born of a closeness neither one of us could bear
I think we had the fault of excessive hope

And were disappointed with time expecting fullness
To be an augmentation of the present more than it would hold
Hours and minutes add up to an inspiration we did not see
And could not endure where you are in wholeness
Time comes to you in floating chunks now and I can see
You mixed in with what is between the places of my life
Eleven months have passed since I began this dialogue with you
Each sentence longing for the entire poem

ooooo

## Sonnet

Head's brain remains the same
So a season unfolds as it goes
By, people speak as a token seek

Remains and wonder what the hell
Or not, so step by step from the bottom
A post sunk in settles, shrunk in the

Weather — an old theme on the borders
Of what we know — our stories all so
Simple, a coupla sentences crumpled

Into balls of paper insensate logical
He has to place himself on actions
Axiomatic at best for the drone of it

That lies within the shape speech made
And follow that content or be disdain

# Precisely the Point Being Made

1993

## What Language is all About

Not about anything at all yet you
Render me hopeless useless to defend
Myself as if this were a fact
So I put on my shirt
Not feeling I've found you finally rather
That you found me. When I am here
I remember you it reminds me of before

ooooo

## Variations: the Path

Each day I walk down the path in the morning and in the afternoon I walk up the path. In the evening I walk down the path and at night I walk up the path. When I walk down the path I can see the little wooden bridge up ahead of me which I will soon be crossing to go down then five wooden steps. When I return in the afternoon I can see the shrubbed hills pushed one against the other, a steep section of blue sky beyond them. Rarely is the sun before me as I walk. In the morning the sun is not yet up. It is dark. Sometimes the moon is up over the top of the large eucalyptus tree. The hooting of owls. In the evening as I walk down the path things are less distinct and quieter. At night it is also dark but it is not as quiet. Every day I can't distinguish any new events in walking up and down the path, and yet I know there are many new events. It is a grade down in the morning and that is why in the afternoon it is a grade up. In winter the grasses are green, in early spring tall and green, in summer and fall yellow and broken. I pass a large house. Going down it is on my right but coming up it is on my left. Slowly the house, once new, is weathering. Now there are two worn lines on the shingled roof to either side of the chimney. I can remember when the house was under construction, when the intricate concrete foundation was poured. Then there were visible changes in the house every day. Now the changes come very slowly. The house is bright in the sun. Every day when I pass the house I look inside. Early in the morning, before dawn, there is sometimes a light on. I can see people moving, talking, in the house, standing in front of the sink beneath the window.

The gravel on the path gradually works its way into the clay, drifts down and through the clay, or washes away when it rains.

*

As I walk up the path I lift my body energetically from the shoulders up to the sky. I pass the big swing set with the patches of grass growing underneath it. I breathe rhythmically as I walk, puffing in deep breaths, swinging my arms. I look at my shoes. I am often carrying something. I think to myself something. To the left, in front of the house, a row of thirsty bamboo about five or six feet high, all broken and mixed up. Beyond that a few small olive trees chewed up by the deer. The boys and girls are playing ball. Smack of hardball in catcher's glove. Sun's out, shines with, I think to myself now, warm tenderness on car bumpers, water spigots, bits of gravel.

There is a moon up as I am coming up the path at night: one quarter moon with bright planets in a line to either side. Over the top of the hill above the small house with the Japanese sliding door and the little porch. A light's on inside. A little blonde girl is seated in front of the window her head bent over her work or food at the table. It's raining, rivulets of water running down the slope just to the right of the path. Wind blows rain crosswise, pops my umbrella inside out, lashes my face. In just a minute I'll be inside the door of the little mud room all crammed up with bicycles baseball gloves old newspapers skateboards and shoes and standing inside, with my umbrella outside. I'll try to set it right and close it. I'll notice one of the ribs is broken. A strong quality of presence. Startling. As if at that time I am not alone although no one is with me. Later on I will remember this and I will write it down. Now I write it. As if in the writing of it I am not alone at this time although no one is here standing beside my desk.

*

Going down the path I pass a little silver trailer on my left. Boards run from the path to the trailer through the soggy grass. There's an orange light on outside the trailer giving light to those who approach. A small wooden addition built onto the trailer. Some big stones nearby. It is not until I cross over the bridge over the creek, now running with runoff water from the hills for the first time this year, that I can see the cars in the parking lot below, there are many of them. I pass them as I walk across the muddy parking lot, squeezing between two cars, careful not to soil my robe against the cars, down the four earth steps and onto another gravel path that will take me to a third path, this one a brick path. I need to hurry: I am late for an appointment. This need to hurry becomes the walking, as if no one is there with me not even myself in the walking. As if the people I am hurrying to see have taken possession of whatever there might be of me for them before I have even arrived. I do not notice the earth colored Japanese house as I pass it. Later in recall I do not even remember to write this down. Someone inside is terribly unhappy.

Going up the path in the morning down the path in the evening I grammatically and so necessarily. Frost on the compost spread over the newly seeded lawn. Because a thought to do so in someone's part someone's mind. Under a grey sky just after dawn frost in uneven patches here and there. California quail and sparrows hop about here and there finding something to eat. The fence beside the children's play yard is slumping and decayed but the little cherry tree in the yard is blooming. I can hear, in my imagination, Virginia's voice, "What's the matter that they or we never follow through on anything, never take care about anything, why don't we know what's important" and I can agree and disagree about this within the privacy of my mind where Virginia is. As I walk up the path past the fruit trees—cherry, pear—bare of leaves and shapely stately standing one here one there in the cold composted field—I look down at my shoes, brown shoes with rawhide shoelaces, tough shoes, well made, a pleasure to watch as they appear and disappear into steps. I will never enter the door of the mudroom, take them off, wake up the children, get them ready for school.

*

I walking down the path pre-dawn. I disposition a bunch of latent likes and dislikes. Everything here. The wooden sounding board struck once each minute, twice till I reach the tree at the top of the steps, whose bark is illuminated by the orange light hung at the corner of the paint shed. Each of my steps makes a definite impression on the mud, splashing as I go across the parking lot, past the dumpsters, to enter the gravel path. Years from now there will be other routes, none of these paths will exist here. In the past this system of paths did not exist. I can see the woman striking the sounding board in the orange light from the fixture hung on the side of the temple building. She's bundled up in a beige woolen scarf and matching hat. It must be cold. Cold constitutes a kind of language because of warm and because of time possibility hope and intelligence. The door behind her makes a sound like a slowly stopping railroad car as it slides, I enter.

Walking up the path I and so. Moon full in the sky just up over the hill. A small herd of deer look up as I come up the path they hesitate, they rush off up the hillside, their hooves snapping coyote bush and poison oak twigs. The garden in front of the little house with the sliding Japanese doors looks mysterious behind the big slatted fence that does not conceal its mounded bushes, moss, and stones. The long grey trailer, under the darkened sky, looks like a battle ship on calm black seas. Again, as before, and again, as in the future, once more this time, some time, as it happens, matters, is constituted, I enter it, he takes off his shoes, sees the children asleep in their beds, moonlight coming in through the wide window above their beds, setting aglow to the motionless heads side by side in the big room.

*

Walking down the path on a bright afternoon I cross the bridge over the creek, dried up now, and sense something unusual. I have to stop to ask myself what it is. While I am asking underneath my words I begin to hear a sound, then it is a loud sound, "buzzing." I look above to see thousands of bees bright mobile specks in the sunlight shot through the blooming black acacia branches above. Spent yellow acacia blossoms dot the flat area on this side of the wooden stairs, some of them flattened into the earth, probably by footsteps. Walking up the path in the morning after dawn, after a rain, all the orange newts waddling to get off the path out of the way of something. Walking up the path in the morning, after dawn, a silver moon in the sky, a sliver of moon in the sky, over hilltops. The lawn is thick and here and there tufts of darker green crabgrass, only a bit of the area now shows compost. There is no longer any fence around the children's play yard and the climbing structure that stood there for many years has been torn down. Two young girls come out of the big house beside the path, walk past me arm in arm. I the afternoon as I walk up the path I see a woman on horseback, English-style, on the trail on the hill above. I the mudroom.

Just after dawn I walk very slowly up the path, my shoes deliberate on the gravel. I watch my shoes as they go up and down, appearing and disappearing. The shoe that is now the front shoe in a moment it is the rear shoe and the former rear shoe now may be called the front shoe, and it keeps on that way as long as I breathe rhythmically and do not do anything to interrupt this on-going walking. In walking I can always see the front foot but can never see the rear foot. I can check to feel if it is there and it does feel as if it is still there even though I cannot see it. This is always true no matter if it is the former or the latter shoe that is the front or rear shoe. The new day seems very fresh. There are swelling buds on the twigs of the newly pruned pear and cherry trees. There is a presence I, look to find the path clogged with California quail who, with gradually increasing agitation, move away from me as I gradually move toward them, until, with a gathering abrupt whirring sound of nearly simultaneous wings accompanied by individualized squawks, they fly away in a direction different from the opposite of the direction I am moving in, but away from me.

*

At night, walking down the path, full moon over treetops. At night walking down the path no moon only two bright planets close together in the northern sky. In the pre-dawn walking down the path I put my hands inside my robe close to my chest and the wide sleeves flap. I am careful when I go down the steps not to catch the sleeves on the railing of the wooden steps. In the afternoon walking up the path I look forward to entering the grey trailer to have a cup of tea. But I never do enter the grey trailer.

*

In the pre-dawn I walk quietly down the path in the dark. I the morning I walk slowly up the path in the cold brightness. I the afternoon I walk up the path in the bright heat. I the morning I walk down the path. The frost is beginning to melt. In the afternoon I walk down the path passing a woman coming up. In the evening I walk up the path carrying something. At night I walk up the path after meeting several people, empty of what was said to the people and by them. At night I walk down the path in the dark mindful not to be late.

Walking down the path past the wide field of weeds in seed. Yellow because of lack of water. There's an old blue bike on its side deep in the weeds. On my right I pass the Abbot who emerges from the large white house carrying a large galvanized watering can. He walks to the back of the house and applies water to a patch of tender green grass in the shadow of the house. To one side of the house, along the path, the bamboo is beginning to push up shoots. The cherry tree among the weeds is in fruit. The cherries are orange-red, not the deeper red of the more common Bing cherry, and they are brilliant, startling red against the yellow weeds, the brown-green hills behind, with the sun catching their color. The pear trees also begin to show the new fruit, small brown and hard, in bunches here and there. They are now on my right as I return up the path just at evening time. Grey fog surrounds, pouring over the tops of the hills, merging every depth and distance into a single oblivious covering chill. Nothing distinct, everything moist. I am still walking, feet moving, arms swinging, I am breathing, the houses before me are getting closer and further away.

*

Two years later I am walking up the path. There is no longer even any sign of the sagging fence that used to surround the children's play yard. It isn't a play yard anymore because the children are too grown up to need a play yard now. Lush grass grows. Early in the morning white points of frost on the grass but by noon droplets of water. In the night grass and bushes quiet in the moonlight. Electric blue flowers on the ceanothus bush behind the slatted fence in the garden in the yard. Standing on the little wooden bridge over the creek which is running full and noisy now in the downpour of steady rain I am very tired out because of all the people who have recently died or will soon die or the many other people who are suffering terribly and there is nothing I can do about this other than walk over the bridge and down the plank that connects the bridge to the earth, the path, going up the path to the house inside the yard where the path ends. I go inside and write this down.

ooooo

## Precisely the Point Being Made

I.

Some of them are left overs.
Some of them are squalls.
I want to make this point.
The bridge cancels it.
Anyone *is* home.
Do not forget to make something some of them want. If they want it it is reason for it although it might only make it a darling tongue.
A sand mountain is not a tongue.
All over clouds renew the daughters.
Politics, we are only just fooling around here.
It is a grand romance really, people, nothing works out, no one's in control.
Since 1985 we know this now.
People will want one.
Gaps and should think.
Solder, to fuse something, in a word, larger.
Anyone would.
Should contain pieces no bigger than this. Confront it.

2.

And it is out of our great misery that we write. Out of a sense that nothing else will work. *We* choose the means and the terms. *We* mine the depths and curl the ends of our tongues. It is like this, a feeling inside that breaks up into words that do not convey thought. Thought is paramount. Six or seven organized ideas at least and we created a dialogue, a theory, that explains our simple mistrust of a way of thinking that destroys: we threw out the whole thing and started over. Afterward we explained it.

What do I mean. Do I know whereof I speak. What did I say. Do I know what I said. Where do I go. Do I go to any place.

Two of them will take me. One of them will take me. Here and over there or in pieces. By the square around it and in the fact that it means there must be an elsewhere we can feel the depth of it.

I always say—no such thing as the present. Only the part, only the past, only the future, squeezing one another out of shape.

Our little lives, like a fingersnap, don't amount to much. Just an arrangement of the same stuff that's always been here, moving in and out of the various combinations like clouds transformed in the sky.

Our hearts alive like a sun disc at the back near the spine.

Nothing to ache for. Nothing to want. All the ones are ones, the twos are twos. They don't know how precisely it's so so they can't settle down that it's precisely so. That is so though.

Birds sing differently on different days according to their codes or scripts.

You know your dog.

3.

They do draw down.

Finish the sentence. If you would wander.

Here's a subject matter, it would lessen, and I discussed with him the situation.

I do not deem this to be so bad if you would be in it a tenderly so forth for me in it and that is why.

How many people benefit because of this.

Speak about it contrariwise that the facts suburb in therefore. I would be a dialogue. I am going there. You will make it more complex still.

Do you think there's nothing to it no shape or size no one in charge no one to take the rap.

Fog has ever been the subject matter. Do you wish to ambition the heart all out of the way for the clothesline maintenance?

Who could possibly be bothered by this? What kind of system would pass this out?

Now is the time to consider a query which is illiterate.

I have several styles depending on the width of the pipes. She made me want at the top but loose hills full of dirt beside Adolph. Six of them at least if one.

The door there would be one to go through, that's how things proceed. Don't walk on down the hall. Up and down. It's not locked, that's it, it's it. It's a false barrier that is why it's impassable.

Don't mention it.

Speak in contrarieties. In darkness light at the end. In light darkness at the beginning. This is why it is always wrong but in this way nothing to be wrong into.

4.

Shadow as the end of days. The fence in the foreground creates it. You can't see the fence only as a shadow to the left of the face, plunges the face into adumbration. Conflagration, warning. You'd as soon a piece of it as anything. To escape from, transfigure, the merely *actual*, making it real. Not a question of language, to explain or describe it, but before the word is spoken nothing is there, and afterward. The shadow often mistaken for God, because it is a shadow small creatures would run away, expecting next a storm to come. But only from their point of view this is the great distinguished thing at last, a voice, not his, was distinctly heard to enunciate. So-called life looming up over the other side of itself showing its real face, of voidness, of inconceivability. Without object, without sentimental conception. Hardly ever can it be said to be in fact here at all in any, in every, way. Beyond, beneath, around through or rather finally *in* psychology. Across the border. All the pieces. Individual souls, great of . . . on which great perfections are if one does . . . in the fulfillment with the neat and pure and perfect—to the success or as he or she moves through life, following admiration unfailing . . . in the highway—Problems are very sordid—it looks as though it were about one thing but actually it's about something else entirely, but alas it is not about that either. The fear of letting go, giving up, bequeathing in the end one's self to a loss of personality intellect and control, not knowing what one feels or how feels, where one is or why. Above all we do need to allow ourselves to look squarely into the face of the gargantuan ugliness that is existence, to face this, digest it, and realize for all its shock value it is in fact only a product of our thought, speech, and imagination, the resolution of opposites. The red sweater that is in fact blue. The mountain that is a lake. The deeply held tolerance of this condition not as a joke trick or indignation but out of reverence. If we had not had a great deal of practice and instruction in putting on our shirt we would have had no idea how to do it.

ooooo

## The Body

The body is nothing but the tendency or the fact of being affected physically otherwise than this there is nothing to be called body besides the fact of the saying itself.

There is affecting physically and the further projection of that which is affected which is not what we mean by body.

Feelings and conceptions project a substance into mind but in reality what is behind the substance is only the activity of feelings and conceptions that occurs in this instance.

“In reality” is a phrase whose referent is a specific problem of human thought or language.

ooooo

Thought’s reflection back on itself gives rise to this problem which amounts to the discrimination of various categories also without anything beyond themselves to refer to.

City’s streets teeming with actual people.

Each thought affects the body physically whether close in or at a distance whether of one’s own accord or another’s.

Hence get the words right but not in the usual way.

The world is constructed of everything that is not the case.

The body is that which is troubled, struck, oppressed, molested, carried off, violated, defiled, broken up. You are prey to your body.

Conceptions are applied as glue to the world to make of things’ negations an outer shape.

When the lion roars mice seek their holes, waterfowl leap into ponds, deer bolt for cover, elephants break their tethers, evacuate their bowels, and run off.

We imagine we touch this shape although what we actually touch is frustration.

The body is affected by touch of cold and heat, of hunger and thirst, gnats, mosquitoes, wind, sun, and snakes.

People impute character onto their tergiversations and get pain thereby. Names dictate us.

That's literature. To name the present would unleash a terrifying amount of force.

ooooo

That's literature. We name the present world in act unconscious, in intention following the blazing shapes.

To speak of this redeems night, waves breaking on the shores of calm.

Harm done and scream to patiently accept is to alter at least cost. This is always an advantage.

Why be unhappy about something if it can be remedied? And what is the use of being unhappy about something if it cannot be remedied?

The body leads on.

(for — and after — Barrett Watten)

ooooo

## The Audience

I have it in mind to produce an effect
That will occasion response
And then various factors again fondly for aggrandizement
You will tell me these things so as to make a heap out of me

This room, very quietly now, only the very slight quiver of thought
You want to get away from it either temporarily or permanently
But there's nowhere to go where it isn't
You want total control over everything
But you already are control right where you stand by the chair
Which is so obscure standing there mute, four-legged, contentious
Is all this amounting to something of an insult.
The whole body, am I reaching you and are you reaching me,
Are you touching the carved recesses, the dark grained and polished wood,
The sense of gravity, confusion's ballast, fruit of location,
Which also did not listen.
These are the principles the method equally clear the result
According to the latest surveys indicates everything's working out as it ought
Our productions producing results at peak performance
Everyone falling precisely into line with the various presents and prizes
Tucked neatly under their arms.
They want to be entertained, even shocked into a moment
Of false and pitiful self-knowledge that will alleviate the disease
That comes from an articulate precise yet substantially incomplete knowledge.
The milk of human kindness.

ooooo

## One Stroke

We write poems waiting for fathers to arise
They breathe into the airplane hangars located in the fiat desert
You are coming into the room over the threshold
Waste, waste and foam, little bits of faraway things on the beach
We are standing before the tallest and oldest tree in the world
That was here most likely long before the time of Christ

When the immense seascape under the wanton sun washed over a sense of
being
That could not be accounted for although it is tucked between the shirts in
the drawer

We cannot profitably plan ahead for our plan strikes empty space
Lined up like container ships forward into time
You want a new color, blue
It is not part and parcel of the meaning, rather it is a feeling
An airplane taking a drastic nosedive over the horizon
Because existence as we know it doesn't make any sense eyes don't see
Age nor distance coming into the room stealthily over the threshold silently
You are there, arising, waiting for poems to be written in explication

Of Christ compared to a bird, a sunset, a fond last meal
Human expression a font for set pieces four eggs a day
The music of wind in trees plays stately down hillsides a front for
Age nor distance is presence dashes forward on the cusp
Of explication and returns hope backwards to you by showing
You a card including the names of all the physicians, I breathe
Into the room I'd enter if I could, ease and peace of mind
The beach seems dirty because of all the amusing things we find on it

You are on your own now there is no help for you nor hope
Whatever completion you expected must be yours by now is an experience
The beach with its nearby trees seems lost, a kin, bones and ornaments
Lace up stock finally, she is addressing us she is speaking these words
At long last, presence just on the verge of mastering the entrance
And clearly we write poems waiting for fathers to arise
But they do not arise they lie sleeping forever just down the corridor
Until our hope awakens them they shamble down the narrow hallway

Complaining of truly insignificant lapses in the arrangements
The car was left running overnight; the butter is too hard
You are coming into the room again, you hardly notice the hard edges
Of the threshold tipping in around your ears, eyes do not see
Though fingers feel the fine frenzy of foamy foolish pieces of a beach
Washed up in an uncanny way-exactly the chance we'd waited for
Sooner or later this tree is going to topple in some storm path
Some blast of icy air and then there is a presence there not quite felt

But somehow sensed walking through the doorway and into the room again
For the first time to cure the sick soul, the sin-sick soul
Of explication, everyone needs a good description of us, eyes do not see
People on the other side view the airplane upside down as it leaves this sphere
The chances of sensible life on another planet in this vast empty universe
Slim sooner or later, fathers complain, this is human expression
In all its color laughter a drafty room for sleeping long sleep
Past becomes future a log burns silent in the night

It is strange, this life in nature, hills, trees, wind on our face
To stand in, be in midst of being all round, moistness none
And some, all and each, rivers, streams, ancient moons apart above else
In a storm there will be a beach so close I can almost reach out and trust it
Loss in the look of loss, an airplane low overhead looks to
People on the other side just exactly right, fathers arise there in the heat
In trees when it is quiet there would be words she spoke and there
Would be those words, the oldest on earth, long before the time of Christ
            at the beginning

Complaining of insignificant loss would be our fate to shut our ears
To calls to give our lives for all the weariness she felt spoken
All out of proportion longed for and listened to on a beach far away
We write poems waiting for fathers to arise they are like trees to us
They do not go away, our life is sealed like an envelope insufficient postage
These are tall ones words to us loss and the look of loss

Yet delighting in the actuality that there is nothing here on the air
A single stroke, black line, fifty pounds of ink, eyes do not see

(for Kazuaki Tanahashi)

ooooo

## It's a Process Based on Release
## And so not to be Taken too Seriously

It is true we can be at two places at once
For the real form of the body is commensurate
With space. A dime will get you one
And there is so much more to be gotten there.
You are in the picture hung up in the barn on a nail.
In the crowd the dancers fling themselves toward the pillars.
The light dims on the cascading beaches.
She would kill and beg for more.
The point seems to be that attendance at the game
Was mandatory. There is no credit for superior birth.
I am going to aid the fire by application of night
While you mount the horse which appears dense
And thus achieves color. Be lost to yourself. Join
The great company of those who have gone beyond this place.
Give up your attempt at hopeful improvement.
Cars calmly cruise the lonely night streets.

Your hair standing all upright this is as abandoned
As the many stages of one thing you are underneath.
Let us guarantee that this one beautiful thing
Will remain here forever on the sidewalk of this
Dilapidated industrial street. I grew up in a town like that.

People there poked their heads out of shop windows
To see a chicken in possession of the streets. Saints
Also felt this in centuries gone by. If you only speak
One language well you are a fool and can't hope to understand
Human nature. In this room pigeons coo and lurch.
There is a pile of money in the corner I will hand out
After you present the right answer. You only try
You never really fail. That is why the contract is awarded
In the subway station last Sunday, millions in attendance.

State the single fact that will give off light
And millions will respond temporarily.
If you are popular and handsome many things
Will follow from this but they are inevitable.
Hope for peace but accept one month's rent in advance.
Line up that way. She presses for your answer
But you are all rolled up into one. There is no
Justice. There is no justice only more of the same.
Flowers jutting out of a crate. The ballplayers
Took the train but landed on their feet. It could only be
The body that affects us this way calling the shots.
Night at last

Isn't it strange that no things are the same?
No two leaves alike, all the hairs on the dog's head
Unique. Approaching this house from your street
You can't help but fall off the curb hurtling down
And calling to yourself at the top.

ooooo

# That Man Died in His Sleep

He called me to say he would be dying very soon
The world is neither soon nor late all its themes
Would quit at a time like this all its fate would never
Last. I think the thought that is the body
There is no question of doing or not doing anything about it
To communicate at a time like this is a delight and a privilege
His eyes looking at me no longer possessed desire nor grief nor even
himself but
Faraway looked like purity and truth, nothing I can name,
From the other side of the grave but grave is not the synecdoche
not what I am
talking about. IT is not death I am talking about.
We always use a lot of words to say what is a simple
thing.
If you are conscious of each breath it is
Possible to be conscious of the last breath after which there is
Not another and what can be said then
There is more desire and less without a body and a house
Without a spouse and many children and the cars to
Put them in in order to move them about
All of this takes money and even after you are dead you still
Have to worry about money
For a moment there is a rest
The swirl goes on piles up things on top that topple
Round and round it goes the voices intoning the endless sentence
Or image of what you'll lose and won't want to lose
I am walking up the hill above the farm
Overlooking trees, fields and ocean.
Almost like that

ooooo

## For Miyazawa Kenji

. . . come to the end of something
would be eternally a matter
of starting over again
as another

. . . in a regularity
at a certain time each day
I take a nap
after which
I walk through the fields to the stable

. . . lost
there is a longing from time to time
for my sister but it's not my sister
I think it must be the waving purple
riceplanttops
under the bunched mauve storm
where the horse quietly eats
just this side of sleep
of which I cannot tell
drowning in my own hopeless tears

. . . everything finished now
the riceplants snapped and limp
not even my words are definite
writing as I walk to visit Mr. Numata
I hear a muffled drone in the trees
continually, a siren

. . . pieces of something not even distinct enough to hold
certainly in defiance of the naming of them
as the horizon appears greyish and on edge

. . . one thing and then another
a storyline without conflict or resolution
each detail brushed on
tiny insect on a page
black butterfly dazed on a fencepost

. . . could be just at the edge of something
about to be in a new condition
pushing the sled down the slope
all the snow obliterating any features
only general shapes the snow circumscribes
the sled runners sharp
cut into the hills of snow
harden them
cold and without resistance

. . . packed
as if years were minutes
tamed
as it's about to become something else
she had the idea of snow so cold and fresh
so permanently verified

. . . lost
the train of thought
the train of feeling sprayed lightly, vaguely, over everything
so that nothing could be found again as such
although nothing ever goes anywhere
to speak of

. . . a window
inside it is warm and dark
outside cold and bright

. . . locking itself
or hearing these are
all the things I'm thinking about
the fire in my chest mounts to my head
all of the time never stops
asking constantly what this
might be pointing toward
any aspiration or hope ("Homage to the Lotus of the True Law!")
you are saying the same thing I am saying
while looking at a mountain of light

ooooo

## For Aldo Leopold

I make an effort to detain myself by grabbing him by the bandage on his
    wrist
    but the yellow hills ruined with cheat fall prey to the flames of
    the times

When you arrived with your fur and limousine it was quite a shock
    to find you diverging from your accustomed state of grace and
    wanting more
    than your usual share
In glades over rivers under peaks inside department stores in major malls
    beribboned with concrete-lined trout streams and real
    corpses wearing underwear

The truth about desire is easy for any school kid to see
    that it is not a matter of what we think we want

But to want what we really want what wanting wants to make sense of
      according to an insight we have one day a long time ago in the present

One thing led to another
      education is learning to see that one thing while going blind to the other thing
It is the heartbreak of the human
      that we successfully fix what cannot be broken and break it
While listening intently to the birds on our way home from work

ooooo

## Arbitrary Subjects

Each time is news, not about what happened
But about what didn't — something

I am writing about I don't know about
That doesn't ever appear in the lines

Can't stop telling about that, a single
Hair pokes holes in everything, an eyeball

Sees, through intensity, mainly seeing but also
Thinking, the sort of thinking that floats

Like a cloud in a big blue sky
Pulling apart and re-forming noisily

One tree top lit in morning's light
A whole mountain of trees remain in dim

Let's start over again again
In an enthusiasm of dejection build new lexicons

To put the world together in a disconstruction
But this time without the ghost that always

Rummages for answers — just the questions
Will do fine — each one stands for a different animal

There's an advantage in not knowing the names for
Anything, and there's a disadvantage

(for Charles Bernstein)

ooooo

## To My Sons

Perhaps after a time
When others review our presence
Our journals bound, strange
That we read and renew the scene
We can't understand without words to
Make it real, adult life.
I could be talking right now
Over again about the script
A red and white camellia in a vase
In the alcove where the scroll reads

"Pine tree green a thousand years"
I throw a bottle over my shoulder.
What a relief!

ooooo

## A Guide

The mind's habits always prevail over clear sight
At the beach. Dire, the world conspires to collapse
Love but it can't do it.
My children are coming.

Here is the true significance of shape: without it
There is no way to form bonds there is no way I can put the letters
in the
Envelope and mail them

They are arriving just about in time. On this day
They are in charge of things all right they place them where they go

I only care, this is the chime, the reflection for which I unfold only
in the midst of water

Along the way up the hill in the meadow there's a cherry tree and the
cherries are
Nearly ripe but there are still flecks of yellow on the cherries and
the color of the cherries
Is a red not the purple-red of the bing cherries but this other brighter
Red that tags the heart surrounded by all that deep green grass
And the green as well of the leaves hanging loosely in the breeze

Can you believe it is possible that despite the quantity of grief
This world affords the tears and pain of people hurting in all possible ways
To make of it a field of bliss and wonder on the skin of that cherry?

I only see the light, these eyes, and dedicate
Form to the construction of containers to hold what can't be held

And the reason is new children are nearly arrived
They do not know and will not stop
This is why they come from water and why the door that is open also closes
Logically at some point in the system you would reckon an end
The cistern would overflow

When I walk through the street moves my boat seems stationary
But the shore moves the shape seems solid yet the light unfurls
From off the blinding figure in the distance repeatedly it flickers and
Grows

The doorway to hell is each an equal and opposite situation
Whether your head's on backwards or your entrails exposed or you pitch forward face first into the flaming soup
Everything results from causes anything goes
and the evil is sufficient to anchor the world

Do one to get one the old bicycle in the yard of weeds
Speech is weeds is mowed and cultivated speech is resurrected
And his steps destruct the malebolge of hell evil powerless
Against good evil wins the deed the double the big spin

For the multitude of uses. It is one fight to reap another to gain
For the spare parts. The house of Nebi Daniel.
What people will do to people the shape can't contain it

Look a ditch and died. Starts out very small but
Builds reserved for us cancelled

A hill the root and trucks protect the house as they had for centuries
You could believe that all the world's ills caused by insufficient
Speech if you like and you'd be right but only kidding yourself
Because the depth of your protest against fragmentation and lies
Will pull you just as deep and dirty as the skies which were once
A metaphor in poetry. Head of the diplomatic corps

And there is no peace at the gates of Jerusalem any more
At the Jaffa Gate or the Mandelbaum Gate or the Zion Gate or St. Ste-
phen's Gate or any gate

He grabbed me by the lapel. "Do you not see?" he pleaded.
Endless work, endless time and space in which to work
Slowly digging with spoons or fountain pen nibs, whatever's to hand
Or to the mind's eye. Ten more minutes.

ooooo

## *from* "Praise"

5 March 1990

My head is cold with wind beating it, head newly shaved for memorial for Maurine, dead these few weeks. Over and over I write this.

Smoke hazy in the air. Edge of sea and sky blur in a haze like the end of all time in mind. People were here before. What did they do. Did they do anything in the way we'd imagine that we'd do, then, as if that time were this, as if there were another time.

Rock so sharp, so clean, in piercing afternoon light, cold winter light. A triangle of lichen-covered stone just up in view frames the farm, as if the farm were there at all for benefit of the rock, as if the rock (which I have either never noticed before nor ever written about before these two and more years) commanded the farm and controlled the farm from above. Farm's green now, all green but for rows of darker green trees, themselves green too.

Dog's rummaging around, after something, who knows what, the air makes him move. Little birds cry.

Sound of flute from far away, maybe by the pond. Pond's quiet. Sea's a blaze of light. Hills go green the eye recoils into a vague dream of green so vivid is the green they touch they cannot define it and swim and pitch glancing off.

Little bushes in bright light and deep shadow.

In the beginning is the ending. If you could see clear enough this would always be clear to you and is always so whether clear or not. To make these words come on, one after the other of them, year after year of them, do they die, do they go on, are they taken and seized for what good they'd fashion and where do they come from and where go. A life fashioned as a consequence of these words. A life that's only a vehicle for these few poor words, dog, pen, pocket, sky, hill, cloud, tree, bird, that have flowed through it only to sigh, falling down the hill and into the blue bulging water.

I do not imagine that many projects occur in any other way than in their completion exactly as they are begun. I go on as if there is a contingency and a possibility for completion, a task and a reward, but actually I sigh in the very breathing of air, in the happiness that the breathing itself does go on as a praise, and a praise in the sound of the wind that cools my head and shirt soaked with sweat from the hike. The wind wants to blow this page over. It will but not yet. Time to start a new one.

My heart is pulled inside out every day. Each day if I look subtly inside there is a mood or a chore, anyway a quest or an attentive consideration, the heart wants to go to a place, and it resists the tasks and plans, doesn't want the projects and situations it wants to go in, deeper, seeing shape there and bringing it on to a pleasing conclusion. But life flows past. We are always forsaken in this.

Waves go back and forth and in doing so seem to be moving not at all.

Sounds of gulls and now the dog barks because of something. But never because of something that can be spoken of.

Curved road leads to the water tank, a circle below. It was built by men. In the dignity of work, taking what wasn't then there and in the conception of it manifesting form to a place. We do this. It is how we speak and why. There are short reasons for it. But there are no long ones. I believe in absolutely nothing, although I frequently forget myself. This is how I come to the end of all I believe.

This notebook goes on really a long long time. And if it ended finally — what then? Would I feel satisfaction, as though conclusion had been reached, a particular shape purified? I don't think so. I am so deeply in now I don't think any shape would signify, any word communicate. For here is where, at the bottom of us, all shapes are one. That there is shape at all. That we are facing it. This also must be praise.

Cars far away that go fast seem to go slow. The many tiny holes in my hat help the wind to bite my head. I don't know where to go from here. I don't know how. A whole lifetime. I am not making a comment on anything. I can't belittle nor magnify society. It is there, somewhere beyond the farm, the true subject of these sentences. Were it not there neither would I. It is to take what I can find here — a brute honesty, an elemental honesty if possible — there, intact, without adulteration, for my own and anyone's benefit. It can't be a question of value. That is a long time, higher and lower than this. It is just this.

Many pages later. The bushes below outlined in light. The sea a pure harmony of light and motionless movement. All around me everything I love. No use in more than that. Nothing to take away, nothing to leave behind. Just one body.

## Some Day

some day
someone
is going to notice
what I have done
then I will know
exactly who I have been
after
they explain it to me
some time
after my death
if I am able to understand

ooooo

## Poem Beginning with a Line from Clark Coolidge

But the sea like the mind owns no lid.
It is clear and knowing but never dwindles.
Waves wave foam and air in fury of froth going forth
Where there is burial of regiment, articulation.
It is only the going, disdain, frequent.

I a single person can be found there weeping.
There is this sort of problem about engraving.
About the age also less to tell than to quarrel with
And even this no more but in crowds of print.
Huge swells, fearful winds and billows.

A concurrent, frequent, coherent image
To which our little boat attaches
Makes of time an inherent situation
An intention wanting direction it can speak with
Soothingly, that is why this table is here for
That is why you should choose a number and wait
Making it smooth
So that you can take your place there in the chair
Next to the table

The table and the chair there
The table frequently there
The chair devastatingly clear
The chair frequently devastating
The analogous et cetera to the table

The chair et cetera the chair
The table condensed to an enigma
The table blended into the chair
Which sat on then systematically disappears
Then without a sitter perplexingly frequent
The chair undistinguished
Unable to bear fruit
Frequently perplexed
Systematically defiant

The chair looks like hair finally
Hair blowing in an ocean of heart
Heart wants ears to beat the boat with frequently
Devastated and panicked in an aura of sight

Eye and chair at bottom like a sigh
You cannot really know why
The storm may come the foam fly

The boat all silver and blue under the sky
Or in the sky no matter how close to which you get
Is not there

I come close to hearing
I come close to seeing
I come close to smelling
I come close to tasting
I come close to feeling

Think I have thought and cannot be sure

# The Narrow Roads of Japan

1998

The moon, the sun, the earth, the stars — everything's always traveling. No way to settle down — every moment's a gesture, a journey, time's shifting scene; a life of such wandering — every place is home. Young we press onward; old we travel back to the places we've been, leading our horse into the evening light. When I was young I wanted always to go. Now I don't much care — but the open highway, lonely and cloud-filled, makes me wonder still. After all, one never really knows where one is or where anyone will end. So, having met many Japanese priests over the years, and entered the lineage, I wanted to go to the Old Country, to see what it was like, to offer incense at Rinso-In, to pay my respects that one time. So we went the five of us — the four to do a ceremony at the big monastery, and myself just to be there. Packed and boarded the plane, I left a poem behind:

> Two countries at
> Each other's throats
> Full of misunderstanding
> And death — two bombs
>
> And a flatness
> Against the horizon's waves
> Between — sitting
>
> Still, wordless, body's
> A grass hut
> Transformed into a doll's house

*

October 14, 1989. Yaizu.

Winding road along coast beside steep mountain. Sides of mountain cemented over, steel poles sunk wire mesh fence hung on steel poles. Everywhere roads are narrow. All the local people at the party after the firing, excitement, noisy, talking, drinking, joking about the wares. Hoitsu made a very large pot that sagged in the firing. I took a picture of him sagging next to the sagging pot. Special ornamental knot made with the tie of the kesa — very hard to remember how to do. So many things like this so many refinements and details. Japanese Zen all about this — religion becomes art becomes identified with the national ethos, what art can do, expressing a people. Then religion as culture loses what religion has to offer — freedom. Happens always. I lose what you find. The way the young girls speak breathlessly as though perpetually worried or embarrassed. So much careful consideration for others. Japanese have small square neat feet. Generalizing about the Japanese. Industrial buildings made of tin, roofs of tin with curved tin ornamental pieces at the end. System of canals. Gohan is rice, what's yelled when the meal is ready. "Go-han!" "Soup's on!" Electric rice cooker, electric kettle on floor next to table on at all times so rice and tea can be served constantly. Konbu, Mirin, Shoyu, bonita flakes, shitake, make good broth for soup. Everything is made of fish — green and red and tan stringy sweet candies. Pressurized coffee in a can. Kohee is coffee. Fire up the boiler at night so we can take a bath — huge metal tub big enough for all five of us. Big blackened beams of Rinso-In. Little places here and there re-done over the last few years. Outside, the sutra house with the big turntable for turning the sutras. Arhat statues built into the hillside covered with ivy and weather. Schoolgirls at the museum in Toro Park want to take my picture. Hoitsu found two cameras in the garbage; they seem to work . . .

Mountains beyond us
Blue
Below yellow clouds
Over setting sun

*

Can't get at
What's there
Beyond the eyes
Sight glances off objects

*

Leaves the body hanging
Asking for more
So the mind
Embraces, fills in

*

With what is
Never the same thing
Twice, constant
Cry in the night

*

Even as I weep
With frustration
Because what I want to say
Cannot be said in English

*

Inconceivable beauty
The mind will find it everywhere
Or nowhere
Depending on the passion of the vow

*

Consonant with love
Tongue flutters
Against great vacant silences
Within distinctions — is the world

*

What you tend to's
What you love
What you take care of's
What you see the beauty in

*

At the time of a birth
A death
An impossible trick
Unexplained by words

*

Neat rice fields
Fanning out around houses and workshops
People's faces
Harmonizing everywhere

*

Those fan-like
Delicate bent
Trees
Are bamboo as I've never seen it before

*

Rice not only eaten as
Staple, sweet, and
Drunk as wine but also
Is glue

*

Undistinguished by either wit or wisdom
Knowledge or the passion of eloquence
I am the one who
Took the time to write the words

*

Proving that
There is a witness
Time has found its collaborator
Someone was there

*

Streets are wide enough for one car only yet the concept of the one-way street escapes the city fathers of Yaizu. Awareness and courtesy prevent accidents and people get out of each other's way without incident. No sidewalks: bikes and pedestrians also use the narrow by-ways. Rain coming down very hard, pounding on the roof and the water in the pond. Covering and homely rain, it will be good for the rice and tea. Rain doesn't bring on cold; it is still warm indoors and out. It is cold just before the rain. Clouds formed all day for this purpose.

*

"Another surge of people
Debouched on them
And pushed them out
Onto the strand"

# Success

2000

## Saturday, 24 February

K's birthday and Fu's birthday
And the day we hear
Maurine and Dainin are nearly dying
Maurine says, Just keep
Practicing
You
Know what to do
As she slips off into coma
For if when we love
Our existence runs through Nature's fingers
Like gold coins she cannot hold
And lets fall to purchase new birth
She now throws as
Without hoping nor expecting anything
In ample handfuls to existence,
Walter Benjamin wrote
And so did I
Nothing is ever gone since nothing ever came
K all day crying for Maurine
Things so clear so bright
When we have come to this decision
Won't tack short pieces onto it
Won't hold back what's going to go on
What always goes on to another place
And in the leaf attacks a small burr
To the edge of a mountainous tunnel
She said something about that once
But it wasn't anything she said that it meant

## Friday, 2 March

I don't think you could do better than that
To write down all what occurs to you
Never mind that you don't know nothing
No one does
They might think so
And everybody says so
But that's just talk
Stand up right in the middle of lunch
And holler or maybe sing
Hit them on the ear with your cane
But love them just the same
Go on as much as you have to for as long as you need
Blood washes out pretty good
In cold water
If applied soon enough
And that soft spot
Around the heart
Could be got at with some kind of special
Wrench
I expect
What you see is what you say
Or was that versa vice?
The seasons have a way of never quite
Arriving like Spring is almost Spring
And then it's Summer but
Something like a stone doesn't look like
It's got that problem
But, you know, it does!

ooooo

## Sunday, 4 March

First Sunday of Lent it is the abstention of time
From appearance, the interior
Of what comes but never goes
How phenomena appear to unfold
Is not one by one.
Compared to a folk song.
I am entirely inside some other voice.
It's just a job is all it is
Covered with soot
It makes a difference
Whether you arrive before the party begins
Or after the game is over
It keeps on getting quieter and quieter
A great warm peacefulness
With nobody there
Maurine said
When she came out of her coma
Just before dying
So today we memorialize her, reading
Rilke, Sonnet from Orpheus
And my own of February 25
Resolving her karma
Giving her final offerings and Refuge
Saying, all of us, how we feel
Chanting Ho for a long time
Then going away slowly
As everything does eventually
All things transient, impermanent

ooooo

## Monday, 19 March

Working backwards
From where the road signs show
A direction
Opposite to the one you're going in
Trying to explain to Monjuvajra
How poetry works and what it's all about
I realize I haven't a clue about
What I'm talking about and he
In his sincere and warm way
Taking it all in, trying to understand,
As though it made some sense
This is a confession, Monju:
I really don't know what I'm talking about
A wonder I've gotten this far
Never moving
From the place where I began
But then my job isn't
To know or explain anything
My job is . . .
I forget what it is
But isn't probably something
Worth doing
Though knowing what it's worth
Isn't my job
Heart's a sea
Flows back and forth
Always moving
Never going anywhere

ooooo

## Saturday, 24 March

A wave or
Regarding Wave
Are titles of books of poets I know,
Great Poets, driving up from San Jose
Freeway like a wave little blinking lights
Of cars, waves dimpling on a stone shore
It is no accident I am writing
Twenty-eight lines a day
According to Peter, Chinese microbiologist,
Who points out 28 days is the moon cycle
And the menstrual cycle
And it is a perfect number
The only one
With two digits
Which means that the total of all its divisors
When you add them up
Equals 28
And not only that: it's the atomic weight
Of the nitrogen molecule
Which makes up over 70% of the atmosphere
We and everything else breathe
Twenty-eight is certainly not an accident
And like everything else in my life
The choice of twenty-eight lines for these poems
Is acutely calculated, deviously well thought through
And incandescently brilliant
It takes years to come up with something this good
A perfect wave

ooooo

## Thursday, 5 April

To find the mind that lacks something
Is to locate something that cannot be found
Anywhere, you can have it in your hand
But it will swell up all out of proportion
Just write a few lines after dinner
Or when you wake up in the morning
This is only to say
That everything is the same
But if you're alive
You discriminate between miso and kuso
Constantly
But upon what basis do you do that?
Find the tiny mind
That you can't put in your hand
And if you can't find it
At least find a way to find it
Or a way toward a way
What occurs doesn't hit a solid wall
But is projected against
White space in color
Hand me your hat
A wild wind comes up
I'm finished with getting slammed
This way and that way against the rails
As the ship swerves from side to side
In the storm
Be sure to leave your address before you go
I might come later and meet you there

ooooo

## Friday, 6 April

All this thinking and writing and
Walking up and down signifying
Something
A long time ago (which means now)
Words for things were those things
And everyone understood themselves perfectly
It all had to do
With separating the darkness from the light
Past from future
Expecting something to happen
You could get
But never did
All the conditional soaked through language
Like blood in a sponge
You can't wear a bone for a hat
But the mystery lies there
A doorway within a doorway
A hat within a hat
So I take to the hills
As guerrillas have always done, hills
Where there are few people but many hiding places
Very few rules
Where at night the moon paints
Silver bushes and small mice run
Away from eagles
Among glistening grasses
I come down from time to time
To see the color of their pants

∞∞∞

## Tuesday, 17 April

Hike to the top of Vernal Falls
As we did fourteen years before
In the rain and mist up the steep stone stairs
Now with our children who weren't then
Scampering up gleefully as we lag behind
And looking out at cliff and snow and tree
Sopping wet and amazed
The big thick Ponderosa pines
Bark all yellow-brown symmetrically scored
On the trail to Happy Isles
Such noble beings as we could never be
Quiet and massively simple
The pinkish clear forest floor so still
Not much to contend for here and not much life
Just enough
As a tributary of the Merced gushes by
This early Spring — for this place —
Where you can see the shocking redbuds all purple
And spiky in bloom
Or the bright red snowflower poking up
Among the expressionless conifers
The dogwood in bloom at exactly this moment
Some white flowers full open
And some still as tiny lively points of dazzling green
On the graceful limbs leaning at angles
To the bigger pines and firs
At the top of the Falls in the loud blasts of spray
A manzanita and a laurel low to the ground in a rock

ooooo

## Thursday, 17 May

Little dogs bark and chase cars
They heap fury onto what transgresses
Righteous propriety and in their indignation
Bring down trajectories of elided hatred
Like sustained subject matter
And thunder rolls in the heavens of the gods
Just don't make any mistakes
You'd arrange, in the midst of society,
That's broken down more or less
Because there're too many people
And individuals' hearts' unexamined need
Has outstripped mind's ability to play
Or pay in the midst of this unknown
Condition to search solution and you'd
Find yourself in the end
Facing these dogs of endless grief —
Only the foolish wish to rule and
Only the greedy are crass enough to be that foolish
No one takes seriously anymore
The possibility of being your own boss
Completely
In the midst of everyone, billions of them,
Involved in delicate negotiations
The contending interests clack amid trumpets
And tear the sky down probably
But nothing deters the energy of these rigorous
Dogs who nip and slash and bay in the night
— pray for a miracle

ooooo

## Tuesday, 5 June

What's the basis of the rules of conduct?
Not that they hem you in
But that they flow like nectar
Naturally
From the clear heart
It's what you want to do
What gives you joy
There are problems only
From the human point of view
But humans aren't human
Only sometimes
And never
No problem but the one you think about
One moon
Or half a moon
Formed by a bare branch
Behind a mountain
And talking for a thousand years
Will never show this
Though we have to talk
More or less like we have to sleep
Or eat or go to the toilet
That's the secret about everything:
It's marvelous, interchangeable
It's high and it's low, if you ask who says so
It's me

ooooo

## Thursday, 7 June

Heat of the day, horror of the night
Placid arrangement and whole hog
Of talk
I become addicted to talk
To the disguise
That is intelligence
To the quicksand
That discourse is that takes me away
From here:
Not that exactly
My dog loves me:
That's what I meant to say
A normal person probably
Should drink five glasses of water
Daily
And I don't mean coffee
I say this
Because I believe
Each and every poem
Should contain at least one
Piece of information
Useful for living
Otherwise why write?
Who am I talking to?
Reading should always be
Careful
And should always be understood
As translation

ooooo

## Saturday, 23 June

Thought, not experiences
Or is it experiences, not thoughts
And words . . .
Are experiences not thoughts
Or are thoughts that are
Experienced
As meanings —
Pure experience beyond words
Could there be such a thing
Could there be ocean without waves
Or waves without ocean
And could I now be
Elsewhere than here
At any other time
No one reads poetry or at least
No one reads my poetry
Not even me
And there is a reason for this
And it is
That it would be impossible
For anyone to read what is written
They are only reading
Air
Somewhere other
Than here
Where the needlepoint of reality
Pierces the interstices of the poem
But this is not the poem

## Sunday, 1 July

Seeing people and seeing them again
They seem to repeat
The further on they get
And it's no surprise
That the dim corner where the table is
No, not that one
Probably the other one
Certainly concentration by which I mean
Holding what's nearest
In the middle warmly
So the voices don't argue with one another
And no incentive
To leave the area
Before the police arrive
But you do
Going up to the top of the mountain
According to the long route
Where you can look down and see
Everything
From inside out
I do not deny that a swarm of them
Would languish and the point I wish to make
Is firmly made
Even beforehand
It gets more and more difficult
The closer to the end
You get
The fewer the possibilities

ooooo

## Sunday, 8 July

The many people arrange
Commas which hardly ever
By design
Appear, commas indicate
A style of thinking that is deliberate
And thought provoking while these lines
Hardly ever feel the breath
Of thought only the hot air
Of desire and the slow fire
Of time's passing on
Into time
In the darkness
Bent out of shape
Like laundry
Hair symbolizes fate
Flowers symbolize delicate means
Parasols the protection of morality
And ornaments the virtuous conduct
That makes a person very lovely
Kathie is always cheerful
Even when she's depressed she seems to me
Cheerful while I am usually rather glum
To myself except when I'm exuberant
When I seem stupid
Beyond this
I know nothing
And my purpose
Is to know nothing

ooooo

## Friday, 27 July

Not a matter of the poem's
Responding to its impulse
Rather the other way round:
To hope to chart or press
Upon a soul in sorrow
Some upward forming arc
The lines carry
And in the fluidity of language
Make a heart that's plugged
Unplugged or anyway
Such is the hope eternal
The Muse dangles
To all her sad and useless slaves
The work of the world
Weighs
More than the total of beings
It's done to serve
And what we get pulls down
Harder than what we give flies up
So that we float someplace
Midstream alas
Probably
Or just a trick of speech and meter
More likely
If you think about anything long and deep enough
It's soon beyond hope
While if you don't
You're sunk even beyond thinking

ooooo

## Thursday, 9 August

I know that my body will decay
That time's ends are not known to me
And its swiftness, like an arrow
Buries me not just later but now
Clouds pile up rain comes down
Finally the entire sky's a sheet
Of dark flat cloud rain slanting
Down in hazy churlish whispers
Onto weathered rock, pines and alpine
Meadow tiny plants
I want to go inside
As deep inside it as is possible to go
Where the clouds are as they move
The top layer East
The lower layer West
No one gives permission for this
And no one cares only they resent
If one walks off by himself to do
Nothing, to sniff the air that soon
Brings rains, desiring nothing producing
Nothing but a hum that means
Nothing to no one
Yet in the end's
The singular thing
Holding up the sky
Fear and rage won't write this
Hamburgers and pie in the restaurant
With big fish mounted on the wall

ooooo

## Tuesday, 28 August

Didn't know exactly
The difference between Elena's poem
Hahn's journal or
Anything else — no mistakes anyplace
Each one
Is one, as Stein said
And
Love what is good
As if bumping into furniture
Andy Levy reminds me that Walter Benjamin
Said that
Nazism aestheticized politics while Marxism
Politicized art
Or perhaps I reminded Andy
By way of explaining how it is that
Heidegger became lost in his thought
Like Pound did
Literally lost, with no sense anymore of who
Or where he actually was
Though Pound
Later regretted this and finally admitted as much
To Ginsberg
As quoted by Hyde
What do you think they are thinking about
When they explain so laboriously Heidegger
Who cannot be explained
Anymore than Benjamin can, at his worst,
Or Pound or Stein or Elena?

ooooo

## Thursday, 6 September

Saying good-bye to Issan
Looking stiff formal and waxy
Like statue of a Zen Master
In white kimono brown rakesu hands crossed
Lying in bed dead
Light wind blowing in stirring curtains
Sunny afternoon — I take refuge in Buddha
Dharma Sangha and
The body of one's self and another
Not two, empty, and
I vow
With all beings
To attain unsurpassable liberation and
Gone, gone completely
Utterly gone
Are some of the things I said on my beads
As a way to say good-bye to old friend
Good monk who demonstrated it's
Mysterious and there's no way
To do it — what? —
Everything, at least twice
According to Philip, and survive
57 years anyway, somehow get along w/out
His dingy who-knows-what cockeyed attitude
And acceptance of anything intolerable
Even making it worse and loving it
And managing to redeem it all
Now resting quiet, complete

ooooo

## Friday, 5 October

Press "enter" in order to continue
Press "escape" in order to change
Into something else
Press "known" in order to freeze
Fluid in the system and to bleed the system
Of fluid press "unknown"
Consider generating
Occasions of fact
As considerations of cloud cover or fog
But relax in the mist
And rain of the presence
Of simply nothing as that
Specific of what can be counted on
With faith
In nothing (which is certainly
A particularly lively sort of faith)
There is random and directed
Thinking coming and going perhaps
Somewhere
Yet thinking has nothing
It needs to do
In that case
Other than to enjoy itself
And purify the ground
Making it smoother
So people don't trip so much
And accidentally smash into one another
Causing an endless chain of trouble

ooooo

## Tuesday, 11 December

I hear voices in my voice
See shapes in my body repeated
That had been there before
Many people are me
Flipped forward and back
As pages of a book
Good burning heart of disjunction
Place
There is none
Though up and down you go
Restless nights in restless places
Not one known
Each returning
A new vision of one
That doesn't match
And not a single one found
That is ever lost
On a cold street under a tree
Homelessness not only a social condition
Result of greed and thoughtless
But the metaphor of our time
Running away from home
Afraid to stop
Because of the thinness of earth
Underfoot
And the transparency of the body
Tried to look for something
In the wrong place

ooooo

## Wednesday, 19 December

Talking to the doctors in the hospital
Nothing ends that never began
I await detention
In an endless diorama of shape
Rain pelts down on
The illegal parking spot splatters
The perfectly usable
Window
The patients are all going
To the same place
Various forms of discharge
Sitting around the table with coloring books
Not in the magazine run by people
Who know a lot about something
I don't know a lot about nothing
It's my one great disappointment
To have forgotten everything
Not to be able to think of anything
Just drenched
And without a change of clothes
I take a hard line I suppose
An identical situation I confuse
With the ramifications of my disposition
Painting everything colossal
And rowing my little boat
Inevitably upstream
Not for fun
But because I am used to it

ooooo

# Slowly but Dearly

2004

## The Heartland

What's outside mind isn't within range
of that royal discourse
philosophy wants to make
words out to be, standing at the angle
light makes shutting up
meaningful thought reason poured from
the veins of that which is —
If God has a meaning people make various
things to what purpose if each thing
has its own face and name
which is never the name we call it —
There's great confusion and eventually
all will keel over and die
to their own experience probably
at midnight on the freezing tundra —
It's not that I want to confirm or confront
but where something calls something stirs
and wants to answer let snow fall
and wind whir to vibrate the foaming shores —
Coax me to sing and I'll sing but

lather me and I'll not elongate
mind or soul, only run about in tight
little circles of light tearing up paper
wondering about what wounds I've made what
worlds I'll conquer — I'm glad when I ring up old friends
think of old times to recall which reduce more or less
to now — Peering into the dark I swoon
in memory and breathe into the space left
behind by others who've passed through so help me
I thematize intentionally poking through lists of words
to take the air out of nouns and actions verbs left finally with

To be
Or not to be
Or maybe
Here's where I trip up and come back to myself
presumably pandering, like prose produced to
describe my day to day ponderous activity
constantly conspiring to withering in the
Heartland, life on the edge, where many of us
keep thinking in what spare time we have
of how to combine two things into nothing —
cold stars on cold beaches —

Time waits for no one nor does it dissolve ever
like so many snowflakes on the tongue

ooooo

## How I Failed in Business Without Really Trying

Is it actually the case, as someone says,
That whatever anyone does
Is a disconscious parody of what anyone did
In a former life in a perfect world?
Could it actually be the case,
That same person argues in a broken world,
That events as we know them here
Are hollow inside, tinny blue, outlined in a tinted light,
Ultra clear, totally lost, and that no one calls
Urgently to you across a moist green glen
Summoning you to places erstwhile or elsewhere —
Only the utter silence you hear in the whine

On the wires or these days wireless air
Where people banter back and forth their superficial
But true business and concern. And how is it
Possible all the marvelous things I've done
To make Chicago a better town
Come ricocheting back at me
Causing my hair to grow grayer and thinner
My skin to sag and the tautness of my thinking
To grow slightly slack and finally goosey loosey and bothersome
While the world goes gray and fuzzy
And the several trees in front of my house
Start to crackle in the heat and tumble down
One by one, like so many glasses of straw-colored wine.
In these last few moments, while I have been considering these things,
Someone flipped the pages of my journal and found note of
One happy day of my life in which all the aspects and shards
Of fitful confusion finally came together in a beautiful clear way
And ripped that page out as exemplary
And the apple trees bloomed pure white and fragrant
And the children again
Counted flowers and found them lacking.
How sinuous is life's road
And how murky life's puddle —
Anything tender and pure just doesn't hold up,
Not for a moment. And here
I am in Poughkeepsie again,
Taking a number and strumming on the old banjo
While I wait my turn
At the pump.

ooooo

## Resounding Display of Categories

Raindrops like strands of pearls
Descend into the gaps make mud
Of earth — I walk in red boots
In the unyielding consequence
There are so many forms
Disaster can take some more clever than others
It's easier to make something up
And stay committed to that and call it
Your life than it is to hurl down
Everything all at once and see stars
Or anyway something blazing hot but slow
Come ricocheting back to blind you
Till there's no memory or thought or
Desire — apparently. Furthermore
(As if this were an organized argument)
If I remain in bed for a hundred years
Nothing prevents me from unlocking
The rivers that flow underneath
My house my hair released my
Quotas abandoned my heart's desires
Augmented to the power of ten
You should see how much all this amounts to
You and all the rest of us should care

ooooo

## The Enigma of Memory

It's freezing at degree zero, wind bites —
The crystal arguments fall into taller shapes

And the tension around the eyes lengthens
At the end of every turn around the park
"Kick Me" is a sign everyone wears
I sidle up to the bar, order trees and sky and limpid waters
Elegantly, paying for the whole thing in pearls
Life goes by like a gunboat, heavy, loaded, and on time
The ankles of misfortune buckle the knees
Of faith — don't obligate anyone, only sew kisses on their asses
And toss the salad of your life
With looming shadows of capitulation
Oiled without gain or diminishment
Every memory binds us to loss

ooooo

## Ingrown

I'm quoting notes from previously
as if surrendering to someone else's thoughts
as if blinded by the paintings of light
that sweep across the room in a day:
chipped furniture and the books that lie
half-eaten in their pools of grump on the
table. No one around to hear me rant.
No one cares to solve my problems.
No one cheers me on
or groans for my protection.

Late at night an empty sky, darkened room —
I wonder whether
more or less threatens me now than before
whether I'll still be talking even after I am dead

or whether the silence at the end of the sentence
after the dense and final rounded period
will overtake me 'fore

I'm done. That's the project: to confirm
and conform, make a strong and full shape,
a job like any other, as the ones one loves
march off in single file singing swaying and hurling flowers —
one must go on cheerfully amidst the many voices
face flushed, arms waving, lungs pumping,
teensy eyes peering out all round at the tunnel, tape, and tin
of weary world's enrapture. Ah heart!
How to hold two things at once in one's hand:
the feeling all's fleeting and the laugh
in the mind to love what's here well
as extremest form of self-defense. Not

only caring, but curing, not only curing
but moving still along, looking for that path
that goes along the river brown with rushing run-off
of childhood and mystificatory initiation,
times of innocence, rude death, and endlessness. In here's
where wonder began which got lost along the way
in an effort to be someone, make use of experience,
negotiate from that position.
Now older (presumably) and having known many others as they've
turned and fired through the numbers
one is used and has been used to tertiary greeting, feed, and
a customary allotment — still the steel
of feeling relaxes all at once and tears
come from nowhere.
Where's portion
to greet pinion
and where's force

to bear
weight of access to open
hefty sealed doors of history's
habit?

Here's about how to prod, ask questions, poke, ponder,
plod on, not wearing one's self out
but laughing too at one's expert advice
and many senses of self-repetition, like daily newspaper,
ever the same yet earnestly seeking newness.
Where do you get to
there from here, how limber up in
advance of waning, when deliver
at whose behest? My theory of prose
goes like this: never mention the
subject about which you speak
never limit characters to specific locations
never end paragraphs with decisive statements and always
render certainties with multiple examples.

The rest is fluctuation.

ooooo

## An Offer You Can't Refuse

What I have to offer you
Finished and condemned
Is a note in a bottle scratched out
In an indecipherable language.
Raising the flag into the cool air
and coming back again to what

no one believes in, no one can even indicate:
a flash in the pan of some sort,
sparks of lightning or from a flintstone,
the sensation of falling and catching yourself
and falling and catching yourself again you sometimes feel
in a dream. And yet there's a way in which
(as we say to one another occasionally)
we do look at each other with a feeling of relief,
as if everything in the world one needed or could possibly endure
were actually present, yet quiet, with a warm curl
of a smile, like the ocean around sunset,
in motion, but subdued and mellow
and about to disappear or at least transform
into liquid moonlight in short order. Our hearts are
worn on our sleeves, or maybe they are pinned
to our lapels like those red ribbons that
signify "Yes I know that many are dying
untimely all the time even as we speak and I
care about it, I'm trying to cope,
but know there's very little I can do."
I sometimes wonder whether I experience anything at all;
when I try to catch it so I can dust it off or stuff it into
a drawer or something it all seems to go cold in my hand
like old smoke that's flown around for quite a while
and has now settled into a little damp powder,
a film on a rock or a log.
Together we can appreciate these things
although we can't ever really know that
or say so
yet we want to
and try
try desperately
to have one another
as something

as such
and fall on our faces every time in the awkwardness of our gesture
or the guttural almost animal tones that issue from our throats
at the behest of our constantly inappropriate clunky desire.
I'm not complaining mind you
or trying to stack up evidence in order to prove my point,
win the case finally, and be declared free and immune at last
with a one-way ticket out of here and $500 in cash.
No, it's just that for better or worse like a lot of you out there
I've taken my seat on that spunky little train that could,
the one that requires you to have a name a body and a form of address
in order to embark, but none of those things do you get to keep
as you get off and find yourself strolling very slowly down the platform
in the dust and flame and smoke with a lot of other enthusiastic souls
equally diaphanous and silent and luminescently tranquil
and there isn't anything I'd rather do between now and the meantime than consider
the question, look at the sky, dot my "i's," cross my "t's,"
and fall in love with all the leftovers.

ooooo

## Slowly but Dearly

The village of day heats the incorporated shadows.
Night falls on the abandoned suitcases.
All around the drastic central fixture
dissonances of fabrication split
the nuances of tongue.
Those who are given to counting count
those to naming name and the rest
flick their fancies listlessly
against the darkened doorways.

Wardens wend the wild weathers
with no respect and no calls to duty.
Dawn dangles itself deliciously
and the women wonder in its warmth.
Now the one thing there is processes
itself widely, dancing like flickers
on the saddening shrubs
running its tiny fingers electrically
ringing statements on its finished foolish
impulses. Dust settles on the round
and dazzling ranches.
All the people
melt down in fortunate praise
which comes off as mellow murmurs
clinging to the testifying trees.

ooooo

## Oh Sorrow of Talking

oh sorrow of talking
like two soft animals
running full speed toward one another
and bursting apart
in a shower of exclamation points!

we only lie down in the dark
and even then it's hard to sleep
because of all we wither at
dying on the vine of a storm

ooooo

# In the Manner of Allen Ginsberg, After His Death

Time goes by in the dimness of cloudy memory
All sheets of muddy delivery an actual person's not
Fixed certainly, changes constantly, yet the shape's familiar
"We do it to each other" makes us hard and fast, immanent,
Look like we're about to appear again as we did before —
It's not that I have to be unpredictable or surprise myself in an obvious
Way but that I can be surprised at any time, admit a light like that in,
So that what occurs is fresh, airy, flexible, ungrabable
Especially the density of emotional intellect, how it's all composed,
Material that's there for it, stuff and thought and identity,
Of this world that it swirls around, big wet lick of the tongue
Thump of the fleshly heart for what happens and has over time —
And all the ones, each accountable, involved, distinct and yearning . . .
Ah, to have a point of view on life and a coherent one at that!
Minimum requirement for poesy? Just another big distraction?
Thoughts flow one on another, and all of them, or only a few of them,
Or none make sense. This is the time to nail down what's indicated
With names — Freud, Marx, Derrida, Genghis Kahn, Buddha, Foucault —
Each a world primitive and mysterious, not any one person but how they
Decorate the line!
In the vast comeuppance known as my life
I dance among fairytales fantasies and wishful thoughts
Up to and including the physiology of vital functions and the autonomic
Nervous system that connects me with all other existence outside
Myself (which includes myself, event, muscle, blood, synapse, language) I
Share with universe all *karanahetu* of me and it
And probably if I could understand the shape of causes (I cannot)
I'd not so persistently ponder the nature of time and self
And so endlessly return in poetry to the fact of trees, the seeing
Of them at a distance, their general shapes and moods,
The way they seem so calm, sentient, and at the same time absolutely

Unconcerned which is comforting and yet not the way I wish to be
It's so easy to become overconfident! To think stupidly
That one's "in a groove," that whatever one comes out with's
Gonna be somehow all right, or accurate, or not a mess
When in fact messes lurk constantly around every corner but why worry?
Twenty-five years of "Zen in America" and where'd it get us?
Just here, where we'd've been in any case, this grab bag of karma, luck,
Confusion and inversion. Planet's future uncertain
At best, doomed at worst, certainly doomed anyhow,
And we in the end, language's bride, sing twitch and twaddle our way
Toward the endless silent happy inevitable fate

ooooo

## Responsibility

Tonight it's quiet or in the quiet
Or, at least, the quiet
Is all around us. What is it
I'm worried about when I
Worry about anything? What is it
I tangle up in, wanting to go home?
From down here I look up at myself
In the little bright square of window
Staring down at me in bemusement
Querying what's it worth. But that's
A question snaps shut on itself
Thoughts with teeth or claws
To scrape away to the very core. What
Cares contains its value, a half life,
Mixed, no doubt, yet fair.
It's always fair or anyway

It's always what's there . . .
And it's not our fault.

ooooo

## How God Gets Into It

God arrives in the transitions —
the times between before and after
the shatterings, bendings, breakings
moments of devilment and blasted pose —
The feeling then arises, a draft in the system
tiny shaft of light in the visual field
which, when noticed and affirmed,
opens out to an aura on the screen of eclectic ineffability —
One's arm open in quietude and perplexity
There's nothing to say, do, or think

ooooo

## I've Changed

I've changed
Shrunk probably
Noticing the prominence
Of my skeleton
This word
I wanted to fondle
That I threw out into the world
That never had a meaning or referent

Except to stand for all I do not know and fear
Now I can feel what it wanted to tell me

ooooo

## The Double . . . Again

I'm surprised.

Like a contract I never signed.

Like a sled going uphill.

Something up my sleeve.

Not that I intended it — whatever I intended wasn't it, was what?

That the people who arrived never really arrived, only appeared to arrive, mingled probably with one another so it wasn't clear whether anyone arrived or if someone which of them separately.

All of it came out of books.

Peeping sheepish the spectacle, which was a confusion although colorful.

Gypsies wandered in all those countries, they came on horseback, carrying bundles, they had bundles tied to horses.

I heard about their intentions, their colorful costumes, their objectionable customs, their powerful voices, they had a sense of the movement and drift, but not the meanings, only voices, and their horses with their separate and uninviting bundles.

They arrived in the various towns they came to, thinking they were the only ones who had come, had arrived in those places, speaking a language no one would speak, so couldn't understand them or say anything to them, and had different intentions, were weary, felt as if they were arriving again at the same place, only this time backwards.

Ordinary people — all of them were ordinary — looking out the window of the wagon — of all my experiences of the world — sailing by in that decaying swaying decrepit way — I am what I'm saying — my own intention — to travel with my uninviting bundle, like the gypsies.

I'm going around — not arriving as I thought I would — gasping probably — looking way way down — into the silences between their uninviting bundles — making some suggestions to them about their intention to keep on with what they were doing before they or anyone else seemed to have arrived — before the book had been opened.

Still the horses kept on.

And I said to him, Suppose you were to stop where you are and go backwards, or go, anyway, just go in another direction, the opposite one, then you would have any kind of idea of where you were going.

He became annoyed at this because of where he was, near the table, on which there's an amber bottle or a clear glass bottle filled with amber liquid, it's impossible to tell which.

The very idea of it was astonishing, that you couldn't tell which, and yet he was annoyed by this in a primary way and it explained all of what was to follow.

I was very tired and that is why I could not keep track of the papers.

Was driven there in a car.

The sun coming up over the edge of the world like one big eye opening startled or in shock at the world at some few secret unintended things in colors in the world and spreading out more light in bands over the water of the world.

Cutting the edges of the water — I must mean words — closely — so that coming into view were many small but delicate things that otherwise couldn't be said to be there.

My work, my contribution, recognition; my erudition, contrition, contention, elation, distribution; my distention, detention, dentition, intention, abstraction; my ordinary inescapable conclusion, shape, the color of me, the single road I'd traveled though I'd lost the map, forgotten the arriving, lost the taste for the meaning or the choice.

The horses pissing into the floor of the very cool night.

Little bugs, crickets, making calming noises into the warm night.

Listless animals, an owl, a fox, three mule deer, aimlessly moving up and down in the night, against the sky with its brambles of interrelated stars.

I intended — I forget which — which of my steps I'd intended to take first — it wasn't correct — I'd needed to retrace my steps, to keep track of sightings, couldn't speak — didn't know whether I'd arrived — but not mechanically — the way it had been before — running late — some other related life — so level, beautifully, perfectly, many of them coming now into the room, startling me with recognition.

I had to rid myself of such notions.

So he said, I do know where I am going I am going from here to there but it is difficult to see in the night and I fall down when I trip on my spurs.

He said, In any case if I roll over onto my back then I am unable to arise afterward.

He said, I'm not sure of any of the colors, the ones I want and the ones I don't want; when I consider what I actually do want I can't answer my own questions, can't make a cry, voice won't, fox, maybe owl, does it for me in the distinct night.

He said, The grasses are far too tall; I hadn't counted on that.

I replied, Rear back on all fours; don't bark though just take a gasping breath.

Is it for mere survival? he asked. Or can I expect pay and benefits?

Only tie up your bundles and go, I replied.

ooooo

## *from* Subject Matter

I: things overheard are subject to interpretation

A cry against a barrier or a backdrop,
a few loose pieces rattling together.

Desire: what I want, or what is me, or what screens me from myself.
That you could lift it up, by a single corner perhaps.

I or me, she, he, it or they, us, all of us, we
not them or it, what designations to repel each other, make borders of connections, refinements, sketches, figures, blueprints.
An official depiction with a significance formulated in thunder.
A cry lingering, patched.
Coming from ... *inside?* ... *outside?* ... *beside?* ...

If we could crawl out to the end of a word . . .
find what there? And in *what manner* to search?
The effort to discover already containing the tragic limits
of dimness.

Lonely.   Alone.   Sole.   Sale or safe.   Stolen.
Consoled or unconsoled, not purchased.
Are we speaking of a condition, a situation, a feeling, or a name?
Finally, a name.
Not someone.   Not anyone.   Not another: or not one.
(For "one" one wants persistently to type "on.")

Empty from the inside out or the outside in.
Figured that way, somehow lovingly.
Fit to be or fit, fitted out, outfitted, and struck probably,
struck with a bright idea.
And there are finally no images that suit it,
so nothing to hold emotion, that I can feel I exist and long
for later, all threadbare and long ago fallen off the loom.
A kind of impassioned waiting . . . for nothing certainly . . .
but full of the experience of, the expression of, exactly
that.

Words not pointing.   People pointing, or people as pointing or pointers, people do not point also (or either) unaware though they may be of such a thing, as pointing, as they desire that to which they point, by means of which they continually sigh is the   speech act.

It can be said with some gesture that can look like certainty
that one is primarily lost, lost in a sort of dream,
lost in an image or a structure mistaken for one's life.

Ordinary object are dream objects.
They are drawn against the dark.
One puts one's hand easily through wall or air, it doesn't matter which, since one so readily becomes the other.
The dark always has perfect follow through, surrounds, blurs
the edges.

A flower, one held aloft with a single trembling drop of dew suspended from a corner of a petal
would be a sham example of that.

*What's brought across . . . ?*
Is this really a question of the actual transportation across barriers?
Is it as bright as one imagines it to be?
There is the issue concerning (concealing?) imputation.
Not disputation, not the two of us speaking together.
What's heard, say, or seen (what's thought or touched) is it merely that
or is there more?

*Ought* to be more.
How did that *ought* first arise?
Is it the equivalent (is there ever any equivalence of any
thing anywhere; how could it be otherwise than
singular and why do we think
of equivalence as calmness)
of *zero* in the organized system of numbers?

I am troubled by all this, or suppose that I am.
Maybe I am only resting, or waiting,
waiting for, say, a bus.

The workers in the control room at the airport noticed an airplane that ought to have left had not yet left but there were signs on the monitors that it soon would be leaving.

This was determined, assumed, and acted upon by piecing together various disparate forms of information in short order.

All parts of a world flying up suddenly coming down, with a mysterious smoothness . . .

Understood as *useful knowledge*.

There was concurrently a debate about *shape,*
whether or not there was
in fact anything that corresponded
to this concept
or whether the sound of one's own voice was in the end
enough.

Hearing it . . .
Which of us could correctly say
that it was heard *(one analyzes the facts presented*
*after having ascertained*
*what would stand as a fact,*
*definitions of that,*
*and then having broken all down*
*makes assertions?)*

How best be what is?
Or . . . is there ever any way to be otherwise than that?
Ever any being other than the one named?
. . . and *what* is spoken of in speaking of that
which is presumed to be elsewhere than speech —
what *things* are referred to?
(Nevertheless . . .)

Hand to hand.
Finger to finger.
Breast to breast.
Better to worst, dust to dust, label to liable.
For all of that and more . . .

. . . an illusion of ongoingness, a stepping forth, parataxis, cheery voice, with tasks.
Heart-felt grief at the passage of time and the plasticity,
the leaded improvisation,
of memory.

Each memory nailing the rememberer to an unknown loss,
to a purported past constantly revised in the dark,
like meeting someone on a busy street,
someone you knew from long ago,
whom you'd frozen at that time
as you now felt you had previously felt she had been,
yet you had not actually felt so,
she had never been so, and no longer was now.

Traffic flowing by in an endless stream;
words written or uttered
with their pauses and significances;
the physical mechanisms of utterance and apprehension;
styles of locution and phrasing from various stages of a life
or historical periods.

. . . but what, if anything, *defines?*
Where, if anywhere, achieve *location?*
Time: there isn't time enough,   we say,
*there isn't time.*

He said, I imagined sailing into a harbor
but in fact my journey merely continued.
I'd imagined a wind to take me there
but there was only the rain.

Something that began
before its beginning
and did not end;
or ended before it began.
No, not anything like that;
the enfolding of feeling
into such limited
and self-canceling words.

# I was Blown Back

2005

A thousand people contained within a lit square
Three trees silhouetted straight up branching eerily out

Ordinary clouds stream against the fluted airways —
How their smoky fingers make music against the dark

Quietly what's good
Descends like dust
Or dusk onto the milky landscapes

The people stand still
And all around them
The bluster of their thinking
Pulls down lightning from above
And the platforms rattle

The owls in the trees scatter their nocturnal alarms —
How decisive the universal defeat

ooooo

In eyes words spill
Thought dissolves in water
Unstable, overflowing its lips
Lapping quiet out beyond the breakers

There's casting up of weight in the swell
So that looking into the depths there's no contact
Outside the sheer warmth that that is there

A presence in the larger vicinity
Is immanent collision

A force pressing over you unannounced
Of memory as far back as the beginning

Carried along in the effortless floating
Sky and sea sketch out an edge
That you reach for with your hand
Making mere gestures within the sounds of the words

Waves sound like tinkling glass on the beaches
My eyes cupped with light so deep back
There's no connecting, no escape

ooooo

How hard I work
To open locks for which there seem to be no keys
Stranded here as usual beside the pump
While the social body blunders on in the forced march of
    its deceptions
Toward a lurching just maybe possible dream
That seems to saturate my soul like starch in a shirt
But always comes to nothing when I can't wake up

No matter how hard I try to assign myself to something
I keep floating free in chunks
Always elusively elsewhere
Which turns out to be a newer version of the same thing
    but in different words
So I can never get used to the feeling of what I am

Still, planes take off into sky
The way you imagine something that might occur tomorrow

That won't quit once you start in on it
Nor blow up properly when the fuse is lit
Giving life that razor's edge quality

ooooo

That love's lidless
Like a tree that falls down all over again
Roots dangling in thin air — the heart's gripless
Attachment

The rain never lets up
Falling uselessly into the sea

Nor do I not speak my mind in the words I employ
Intending to go left my letters veer right
Fall in lines where I wish to rise

The body takes no orders
Its nature is to be disturbed
Molested, corrupted, folded
Into a priceless perfection
As the motion of a wave

Released like the spray
Hazed out in minute momentary droplets
By the force of a breaker on a rock

ooooo

Time goes slow when you're desperate
Someone throws one fish into the boat, flopping
And the imaginary dream-worlds you usually live in,
Gauzy structures like sticky webs of time
In the middle of apparently persistent objects that wave
            among them like seaweed
Dissolve in a farrago of groping limbs —
Ah how hopeless it is, this haystack search
For the bright needle of self restoration —
Like rehabilitating an antique table, over and over you buff
The past to remove stains and scratches, produce a sheen,
But it's not working: memory's a deception
As is any organized notion of the person you are
That falls with the weight of what happens
Should the organs of perception ever actually tote the heft

. . .

What was that I just saw swimming by?

ooooo

Because you expected them
To deliver what they seemed to ship
To match an inspired but contorted vision
Cloud-like in the world
You grow dark, disturbed
Stalk long corridors close to walls
Dart outside buildings
Into cold streets
Constantly mad at the sky —

It will take you years to learn
Words are free of their intentions
Fluttering like flags
They are more hymns than contracts
Though they are never without promise

ooooo

One life answers another
In the long conversation that's falling
Through the timbre of our reedy voices
Endless calling and answering
Like circulating winds spelling out our names
That later on we forget
Just when we most need to know them
So as to hold a world solid
But by then we no longer care
Because we're swimming,
Swimming and floating
And shore is just a word we thought we knew
Sibilance of wind calling us onward

ooooo

Now quietly I think of learning
Flinging it out all around like rice grains
Like music on the cornet

If a soul's like milk to be poured out
Why not lean forward into it, letting the quiet

Absorb the tatters of the memory fabric
That will bring you back to perfect place
As if it were a verb tense wreaking havoc
In the breasts of beasts and birds

Such small hearts flutter so quickly as they pass
Like angels addressing our meals
Little perfect eyes amassing evidence
For some global argument deep among the throats

ooooo

What a luxury it would be
To have an inner life
A few trees in a pot
A scrawled list of formerly used words
And music, plenty of music,
That tinkles down the stairs like water
Or tiny shards of ice falling off melting roofs
Not to have to worry about the many arrangements
That go to shore up a life
It would be a pleasure to sink into those waters
And there would be no more images

ooooo

The air talks to me in fluttering words
Birds in their patterns of flight
Earth underfoot relates her old tales
Reading these lines I crawl out to their edges

And gasp, returning, to be held again
In thrall to further thoughts
That fix my weight like a wire across the abyss —

Human mind's not human nature —

Looking out at landscape I hear the songs

ooooo

How I am is simple —
Just a word
That things roll in —
I know that
It's the shape
Their echo, reminder,
Their endless gentle streaming
Rocks me to sleep at night

ooooo

Being old isn't —
The bodily sensations —
Are pleasant
Unpleasant
Interpreted in reference to memory
Obey the social contract of age,
Agreement, designation
Imputed on reading a face in the mirror
Which with advancing time

In reference to a fixture in the soul
Of self's melodious repetition
Is an object of questioning,
Searching look in eyes' brightness, chin's slump

All ages persist as one always
There's nor old nor young but additions
In the inventory of resignations
In the fact
Of the face
Or as the face
The silence in what comes and goes
In and out the opening

ooooo

You opened the gates
To speaking
So distance swallowed you —
The dangling words
Like columns of smoke
Ascending

Not trying to build a boat
Or threaten with a jawbone
You didn't materialize as someone
Which is a relief, only the body
Like soft fur pulsing
Constantly undulating air
Like a silky water-helmet
Flowing cool over a rock
Moves constant through the mist —

Being that but not knowing it
So you could say so
Other than jabbering
Broken-open syllables
Which sound beyond intelligibility
You pass through singing

(for Philip Whalen 1923 - 2002)

ooooo

Poetry's a way not a topos
In which something appears —
It's a sway among a swarm
To be hurled from side to side
Against the language walls
That tunnel subversive
Through what is
As far as it is known —
Occasioning a gap in mind
Through which you could theoretically drive a truck

Meanwhile dogs bark and canaries tweet
Monkeys propend opposable thumbs
The covering sky won't shake out its stars
To cooperate with the head's coolness
The disaster that is human life on earth —

That this can be said (imagination
Blisters in the cauterized night)
Is possible only in the reams of paper
These hidden significant blotches of ink

We twiddle in the dark —

I know my fate rests with the embers

ooooo

I hear the sea washing the sky
Combing out the clouds' hair
As your hair is combed
By the beauty of your thinking —

If you are unsure
Do not shear — leave the camp
And in the desert ask
The important questions
And see who answers
When the bitter flavor trickles down the throat
Dissolving in the stomach's darkness

ooooo

Forgive everything because nothing prevents you
From being a person — they only aid the cause
Gathered together in the twilight
Where amid the ringing of bells
You stop what you thought you were doing
And hold forth

ooooo

## *from* Ask A Difficult Question

Variations on Rumi
In memoriam, Anne Wruble, November 14, 1947 - August 28, 1999

2.

*Days full of wanting*
*Let them go by without worrying*
*that they do.  Stay where you are*
*inside such a pure, hollow note.*

Memory redactions are the mind's music
In the mind's mirror reflections of what's wanted, what is
No images
Only a smell
Of childhood
No one's parents
Coming along behind in round black cars
No one's photographs
Old clothing retrieved
Wanting is longing, distance
Means what's close appears far
As reaching out one's hand toward fruit
What's there recedes, disappears
(As the street curves
(As the old brick school
(Next to the white church
(The children entering
(In a freeze frame of long ago
Just remaining in that sound as if a bell
The present not disturbing the past
Settling into it like something falling into duff
The feeling of the ending included in the beginning

Everything mechanical approaching distance like a bell
Pure tone, water tone
(Road rises up behind the house
(Car climbs against the flat road and the hill
Journey, movement
But no characters
In the story
No forgiving framework
No persons, no personalities
Only struggle in the red tide of desperately
Losing what one built up
Like the water that rises falls back
Crashing
Against the thrusting up of the land
Taking the town and the buildings with it, streets
Buckling
Leaving debris and mud and breakage in its wake
(In the dream I wake to a feeling
(Not images only the feeling of the road climbing
(Humming sound of the tires
(Feeling what was incomplete
(My hand reached out for it but it was
(Dim, churned up, bloated fish floating in it
(And I could not advance only reach
But now there's something in it
The past isn't behind
Rather is mixed in like a color of paint
(A hump in the street next to the railroad track
(Beyond it the hill covered with trees
Some of the places I remember are gone
Encoded only in the body
That was the ghost they were
So that breathing the shadow
Those places grew brighter, reemerged

But the person speaking to me
Is gone as if she never were, also a dream
Her voice a mumble, can't make out words
But sense the speech as true
In the book those are the same words in the note
Words recalled
Or were embedded there
Black letters flaming on the white page
Indecipherable yet sweet
Farmland in gentle hills a code
The square fields in colors a code
The dividing trees enforcing a code
The only place to be in the words
As if the black lines
Crawling deliberately across the page
Were place enough
Persons whose passions are a code
Remember this
Suddenly flaps
A linen sheet or a cloth
Covering it so it's seen only as shape
That remains in motion
Unrecognizable only one knows it is there
Beneath
All what we speak of
Cleaning the table and the floor
Again
So many words again
Bodies and feelings again
Making something out of the world
The battle to defend the river
The fort that stood two years
Guns blazing and finally burned
(A stone marks that place

(Erected 1900
(As memory in the wedged corner of a front yard
(By the house on the river
(You go by there but do not know what this means

5.

*Whoever acts with respect will get respect.*
*Whoever brings sweetness*
*will be served almond cake.*

Love is determined to find its object
In the things scattered about the room
Dolls and photographs
Covered furniture
Ceramic statues unopened mahogany boxes
Clothes in the closet keepsakes in the drawer
Like an open space by the bridge across the river
Not thinking about it but receiving all that's heard
The old remember the long past
In stories
In tales the tragedy recedes
To become a telling
A respect of considering
The ends of stories, power toward which the mind
Inclines, entanglement with focus
(As a scattered light comes in gray in the morning
(Because the back room's enclosed
(There's less light so the room is more quiet
(Left to one's self a music of intention
(That the past — by the big chestnut trees
(Under the snow tunnels as children we dug
(Or the snowmen, we played at having a store

(Because everyone we knew had a store
(With its merchandise to be counted and exchanged
(In that weather at that time
And they believed in the words that reminded them
Said, Pay attention to what has been told
To what has passionately been repeated and sung
What has been sounded out on trumpets
Pay attention to that
When you come in and when you go out
By your arm and on your head
Do not imagine or construct anything
Because you cannot make anything that is not tainted
By wild desire, it is not new
Running along another road
But remember the story of what's been repeated
In the comfort of authority
Be bound in that for the goodness it brings
Being a fine person is that
Held in the flaming words
Of how you are, be that
In the town create people to depend on to use
For the going
Of the entanglement of where you are to go
A white piece of cloth
Only knotted that way
Call it a name but do not say the name
Know it but do not think of it as a name

6.

*I can't explain the goings,*
*or the comings. You enter suddenly,*
*and I am nowhere again.*
*Inside the majesty.*

You enter suddenly
And I am here again
In a familiar place
(Rugs and a window near the sea
(Openings and closings of the heart
(In the fabric of tasks and relationships
(Ideologies and mutual understandings
(In the early morning quiet, swirl of sound
(Or thought or memory
I do not know how I arrived
In my dream
I stood looking
Only an eye, yellow
The crows in the cages not to be trusted
Ruthless they would peck out an eye
And to them it would be natural
In the teeming market to be careful about what to touch
Or who to stand next to
In this place that is home
Suddenly you're not there
Only if you return
After many years
(In that place
(Which recalls
(Your thought
(Emotions
(Like fear or confusion
(Simply not knowing
(What something meant, that large lawn on it
(With the tall white statue of a comforting Jesus
(The church had placed there — it is still there
(The opaque majestic presence of Jesus a vague threat
(Although normal in someone's world

So it is every day an ordinary world
Then not
It is each time now an explainable sorrow
You do not even think of it, it has a date or a place
Then not — it may erupt on you or it may not
A fragrance in the clothing you are wearing
Or a sheen about the edges of hair
A shimmer in blowing leaves
A stone with an inscription on it in a graveyard
(The person not yet dead but wishing he were
(Making all the necessary preparations
Because death is unexplained
All your life looking over ordinary things
For the opening
In creases or worn spots
Precious stones or objects of desire
In flesh, in food, in flashing images
Always imagining something edged with the look of things
Bordered or crossed, etched or gouged
(Like the time something you had you wanted
(Disappeared suddenly
(Gone utterly
(And it would not return
(No one would make it
(And you felt tears
(Of injustice and loss
(And anger against the hardness
(Of the container of the world
(You knew was not so — and time made that
(Also pass —
(So now speaking there is awareness
(Also of that, it can't be memory
(And words will not speak to who it is
(Other

(And only also
(Myself
(Other and one, another or the unknown one
(As one as the called out to, the named without names
(The never answered
The vegetation's proxy and the furious stone's song
Gapped and fluted borderline dimness
Going around the earth and among people
You cannot be sure of knowing
Cannot plumb the syntax the signs things are
(Some do not believe this
(So many ways to approach the seen
(The sensed — how large to make it how subtle
And surprised you got a grip on what matters you made
Boring into it falling through the hole
But the love not for anyone but everyone
Do not speak of any person or sing psalms
Only stand back bathed in that light
That's not named

10.

*Close both eyes*
*to see with the other eye.*

The wise one utters words
But his heart is not stolen
Words are like rocks on a mountain
Therefore you cannot pick them up
Do not hurl them down
For they might pull the mountain apart
Or smash something below
And the splash they make in the waters

When they fly into them from above
Will reverberate too strongly
In the ears of animals
So memorize words engrave them in the ear
Do not allow them the room to be held
Only float by on sound (Music's made
(Beyond the flames of remembering
(Words in the book where you live
(Set to melody they kindle the fire
(That melts the hills like wax
When you arrive remember the landscape
See the sea surrounding the edges of the land
Without crowding it
Coming back again
With great power yet only going so far
(No, sea engulfs the land and eats it
(Land disappears into the sea
(Fire eats earth and it disappears
(Small burnt stone circling endlessly
(In space
Who can draw
A line between
One thing
And another?
Who can find justice
Smudged into that line?
The hole in the heart — fall into it
Forever and speak of it in all that you say
(Words concur with sight,
(Sound, definition's equality or identity
(A cipher or an enigma
So that we can stand down or up
Inspired to form cursory words
Rocks around which waters stream

In the primary sources of the syllable
Letters arise from nowhere, neither body nor mind
Having no form they arise without basis
Instantaneous things hollow and false
Without maker, arising like smoke
Within and without fire
Icons of what is
History and memory together — odes
To perception and the incandescence
Of experience, the "you"
In the "me"
Called out inutterable
In the rock that makes the waters move
In another way, creates a white fury
Where otherwise there is none, place for stalling
So order is imposed
And my foot slips because I do not see the reason
My hand turns against itself
Because I cannot uncover the sky
What I am and know
Flows from what is not I fall
Into the animal
Rise up into the vegetable all days
Reveal and unravel themselves
As the first, as the initial order
Like people wearing gorgeous clothing in a city
Where streets teem with the burdened poor
— Now close the eyes
— See what's on the other side
— Of desire you cannot bear
— To look at

28.

*To change*
*a person must face*
*the dragon of his appetites*
*with another dragon,*
*the life energy*
*of the soul.*

Waves of what went before's momentum
Slosh onto the shores of now
Just as a stone dropped from on high
Will fall
Till it lands
So my passion's
Not my fault only I can
Let it fall
Not bat it around too much with a crude club
Till it beat my head
Unconscious
Desire rises up and falls
Life's pulse and flow
Makes beauty to be in sensation
All void and gone in the peaceful doing
Of what's so in a life in a time and a place
So all desire's satisfaction of itself
To be enjoyed and followed
Not as what's grasped and poked into being
(Which never can be but only a thrusting
(Rapping at the door that's only opened
(By a free wind gently wafting
But as what floats on mind's waters
Anything the senses mend
In sensation pushing or thrusting aside

Holding what's thin air
As if it were a knotted cloth
As if a thread to be followed to be woven into a garment
That couldn't be but only crashing necessity
Weighs down, old mistake
Never stopping any of that (all the words
(That came to me that I want to let them
(Come to me that they can make a circle
(To be closed knit time past to be present
(Bridge future in the darkened windows of time
Only allowing the openness of it (like a door
(Open and you can go in
(Shutting it behind you
To enjoy itself by putting aside the luggage and the broom
Making something quiet in the room
So that the sound opens as the soil opens
And you can plant
Darkness

29.

*Every part of you has a secret language.*
*Your hands and your feet say what you've done.*
*And every need brings in what's needed.*
*Pain bears its cure like a child.*
*Having nothing produces provisions.*
*Ask a difficult question,*
*and the marvelous answer appears.*

# Questions / Places / Voices / Seasons

2008

## *from* Questions

### Pardes

The trees bear fruit, the book
Binds
Like water brimming in the pitcher's
Poured out steady till no drop's left
By a firm hand, an outstretched arm,
The book bears them on through the storm
Tree tops twisting, stripped debris shattered
In the violent nights
Though the fruit's sweet lingers on the tongue
Like melody —
That's the plain meaning

Beyond that and embedded in it
Like seeds in a winter earth
(Officially only a thin layer
Atop a hard dark mystery below
Exactly as deep as the plow turns)
The meaning-fingers splayed forth
Like hairy roots laterally
Entangling other letters, heterodox tales, bits and strands

(The third level now)
Of lives, songs, opinions, certainties
Wild stories, rewordings, revisions
Attempts to harmonize or humanize
Upheaval, sickness, fierce mistaken force
The worm in the infinite, how sky
Reflects the turmoil of the sea
The soul's own sequential poisoning
In its reversing desire to crawl out

Of its own skin, like the famous snake
That spoke for it in the orchard
That had no hands to touch with, to grasp

Then the inner turning
The quiet of snow falling on rock and twig
With a hush beyond speculation and thinking
A meaning pressed only into breathing
Or illuminated by the speechless waters
That suck underground
Into the capillary rootlets opening beneath the feet
In the winding uncharted journey of footsteps
From one point of darkness to the next

ooooo

## *from* Charlotte's Way

It begins and ends here
Not in the body, too gross an exaggeration,
But in the house, like all monuments fleeting as stone
Restoring the forest floor to scratches and lashings
"Nor any pure light" — that's desire
Outside see the sky masticate itself
Inside see the empty boxes full of things
That have been disbursed throughout the heavens
Rapidly, rapidly, without anyone ever having looked at them closely
They flow, like drapery or soil
And each one possess the confidence I lack
Knowing it holds in its fullness in thingness a rightness a weight
Kissing and kissed by the ground
Each falls according to rules and does so willingly

Whereas I hope to escape the house in literal flight rising up into the air
like laughter
My every thought in exact defiance of gravity
"Sunlight all year round has just suffused the dream-filled branches"
And "I'm a bother, cumbersome leafy branch you drag along behind"
Heavy it's true as it obscures all traces
Like a storyline pursued at the expense of perception
So many things have already happened
You are not gentle enough with yourself
So I must be harsh with you
"And where is the world without you?" you ask —
There where it ever was, a snow-covered pine in the midst
Of a meadow, the thick silence following the tortured music, spring
Then autumn, winter, summer, then spring
So you stand forever just inside the green door
Dressed in white
Against the background
Your hair also black
Black your hand resting delicately on your breast
Vivid in the detail of its etched lines and the caress of its nearness in light
As you look down bemused and absorbed at the sign that reads "Please knock"
Your nose wrinkled into a perfect wedge by sheer effort of your timeless smile

*

Your nose wrinkled into a perfect wedge by your smile
Reduced now to a memory dancing on the wings of consciousness or light
So mixed in with nearly everything, proffered as a reward for being
Or for having been a while alive
Still, things pile up and today the sky's creamy foggy, pressing down upon
the hills
And the sea's still urging onward, skirting up against dramatic rocks
Sky sea and land meeting at the edge where we are
Always standing hoping gaping or gasping

Where trees or rock stand fast against the gales now rooms
Protect thought so produce such lonely words
Product of all those deaths from the past
And the chattering swirling round them, a parade of images and keepsakes
How does the floor feel now? Allow
Your eyelids to be closed
This not thinking about it is a good clue
Is the glue for the curiosity to go far out there into waves
Drifting out past the surf, hear the whisper and peace in the threat
Slowly winding down till there's no more —
A tent in time moved constantly with the desert storms
Becomes a house, a construct, a metaphor struck
Into the earth like bedrock
It's got to be fed with smoke and flesh
That eventually curls round the earth and horribly back to you
As everything comes back to you in ways you could not reckon
There: at the top

*

There: at the top
Where music swirls digesting all the images
Even nothing to be said or felt, melted into it
The flesh is that, a house for the fleeting impressions, sea
Of magnificent awareness, is this concrete enough?
You can see my back when I flee into the distance where I belong
But my face (that glows with smoldering light, smoking coals, tongues of
flame)
You do not see for you sleep — sleep and dream
This world, your life, your house constant
In need of renovation — all the world's activity
Maintenance, the continual pushing uphill against entropy
A function of the speed we move at, slow oxidation —
Stuff's burning up — a fly buzzes by — they still play Bach

Even in California — it turned out to be not a towhee but a
Canyon wren (not a bushtit): so one would naturally come to the question,
Is there a state possible in which we can be
Without watching and judging simply awake?
"My body is only there to carry my brains from place to place!"
And so yes of course you arrive there, where you were fated to be
It comes after long journeying, dizzying flight
Acres and acres of mud
Swirling waters with leaves and tree branches pulled along, debris of
Smashed houses, drowned animals
And there you are, just at the point of begin

*

There you are, just at the point of begin
The continuous nerve movie always starts in the middle
Going out from there in several directions at once — pleasure
Of finding out what your life is or was, always incomplete
Just at the point of understanding something but not yet understanding
And important because of faith

*

Important because of faith
Sum of all word, thought, deed
Swirling cloud and water, which moves according to air
Warm or cold because the planet's tilted
Sometimes toward or away from the sun as it journeys
Which is why birds fly south and how
Return initially to the places they left
Because the days were longer then
Yet I, in my house, putter — I put many small metallic things away
In the places where they go
Slowly moving through the diverging rooms

As rain deliberately falls — how much more
My life has been than it ever was and how much less
This sentence is than anything it undescribes
Ghost of my face against the pane
The chairs against the table stand ready
The silent pictures on the wall
Hold their peace in the rich neutral light
Like Morandi's bottles painted into the background gray or white or an
indecipherable green
All but erased into what surrounds them, an almost final swoon
Into undivided life — is this for or against
Inside or outside
The house?

*

The house —
Abandoned faces when the music's faded
Leaving only the thick silences, or silence
(Can silence ever be plural, different, or is it always only just
Mixed with all the music we make
In living, endless living symphony of being, the one silence)
Loosely or harshly held in place for a moment
That returns to shore always eventually
Only the pace and thickness vary as the elements
Recombine — a whale breathing in a rough sea
Has difficulty taking in air that's not
Also mixed with water so must time a leap cutting across a wave
That might be several stories high
Smoothly which is easily done but not furtively, nothing
About a whale is furtive, though a pale lizard running up the stucco wall
In a hacienda in Mexico is furtive as is a cockroach behind a plate
A bird flutters always looking about for it is
A small creature, lives fast, burns

More quickly than I do does not as I do
So willfully forget
I depend on forgetting in order to remember
What I need to know
So I can arrive just here at the spot
And know myself exactly enough to meet you

*

Exactly enough to meet you restlessly
In the shadow of forgetting
Which occurs so quickly and in such detail
Even the tips of the cypress trees subtly quivering in the salt wind
Know of it and reflect it in their patterns now yielding
To another now
Under equally changeable skies
As I write this line a leaf blows by

*

As I wrote that line a leaf blew by
Which I'd've forgotten if not for
Writing which makes a new now frozen
And not frozen in a reader's fluid awareness
A face, or faces, a face is always plural like a sea or a sky
For clouds or waves just as surely roll across it
And light does too
Though there's nothing to be fixed or retained
The face expresses a person, a feeling
That is a person each face a history
Of a reckoning and a history
And a request consented to
With courage making a singular life story

Journey on the seas back to an island
Bright in the sunlight

*

Sky's not bright, it's creamy, gauzy, unsettled
Dark clouds scudding across and seas that mount and tumble
To recognize emotions but not create them, to open up a crack for time
To slip in but not weave an elaborate trope upon it, not make it into a boat
Or shopping spree — lurching toward subject matter — a reflex common to all
You're shocked to see what something's really worth, in a gallery
The priceless paintings are priceless but more priceless is the precious person puzzling over them
More distinct, all her history etched across her face
You didn't give me an answer for why my tears came
And then later when I saw why that was I felt more emotion than ever before
In waves came over me. Like a pelting rain —
Could you speak it out, express what you feel not later after you'd not for a long time
Known it but now, as you feel it, let it flow clear through
As words are windows onto sea or sky
Though there are no birds flowing now across sky's curtain
There are always little whispers of contentment
And a long times goes by before you hear them
Beginning with the bottoms of your feet
Let me give you an example
A man had a shoulder pushed up
It was because his father had beat him and he would raise his arm to protect himself
But now the father was dead and yet this shoulder tensed that way
For to be ready to be attacked all the time is to flee from one's own body
And not to let the past have its decent burial
Why does the single cypress branch shoot up like that high and green beyond the others?

Not a street to be seen, not enclosed within a house but washed
By sea a wind sounds, everywhere alert
And bracing — this is after all just one of many
Possible planets and all unfolds here according to what can be named
One after the other, starting with the waters separate from the sky
Speaking the world to be: "world," what's
Meant by that if not a namelessness
Utterly to be depended on?

ooooo

## *from* Voices

## After Alberto Caeiro (1)

I'm a shepherd grazing my flock
But it's a flock of goats not sheep
I am therefore technically a goatherd
Though I have a few sheep
With goats there is only the milk
And then the cheese, some flesh
Goats are not picturesque as sheep are
They are not so helpless or docile
They are troublesome and contrary
Given to eating many things that are not good for them
And to biting one another aggressively and without reason
When tethered my goats become wound up in the tether
If I allow them their freedom
And follow them to where they are going
I, with them, become lost in the thickets
The secret obscure places
They somehow manage to find

Though I know they are not looking for these places
These places find them
As a consequence of their own goatish willfulness
That seems to be as indelibly their nature
As talking of them seems to be mine —
If, as I say, I follow their entanglements
I become drawn into their dreams
Until my beard becomes goatish
Wiry and full of roughness
That not even dutifully applied oils will smooth away
To me, goat meat is foul — nothing like mutton —
Barely edible; I would prefer almost anything
Except coyote or cat which are worse
So I do not slaughter my goats nor sell them to one who would slaughter
Because it is too much trouble to find such a one
And I do not have the stomach for that sort of searching
Nor anything for which I care to trade
So that when a goat of mine grows too old to breed
I simply stop paying attention
And this goat slowly leaves the flock,
A little more absent today
Than the day before
Until finally one morning the goat is gone
Having faded entirely away
Not to be seen again
But remembered faintly as an odor
Hovering over the brush and grasses
And is not missed
Goats do not make good companions
They are all mouth and their bodies seem forever to be straining
Toward something they do not find
Nor even recognize, a useless painful straining
With nothing elegant or noble about it
Perhaps their mountain ancestors expressed something of animal nobility

But the goat wedded so long to the human
Made brute by doing our bidding,
Living in our houses, feeding our children
Has very little to recommend him
His smell so unmistakable and sharp
Has accompanied me these many years
Until it has become my chief thought
And it has become as well
The smell of the plains and buttes
Even of the bushes and grasses
Even our great cities
Where merchants gather with their exotic wares
Brought from abroad
Now smell of goat
Beneath the many other odors the cities contain
That are far preferable
Because they make us feel sophisticated and worthwhile
But one can't escape even there the odor of goat
Hanging on the air, the basis for all other smells
People jeer at me because I live with goats
But I am not troubled by this
Are goats worse than cows or pigs?
In many ways they are better and easier to keep
Besides, my goats, though unintelligent and unpleasant
Possess a certain goatish integrity
They do not linger enviously
They do not dissemble
They are not insistent
They do not whine they bleat
Which is a stronger and clearer expression
One which requires no retort or response for it is already complete
Goats play out their goat destinies with a pure mute passion
That I appreciate
And although I do not love them

At least I see nothing in them worth hating
Which is more than I can say of people
Of whom a few
Are worth at least
An indifferent sort of antipathy
And in this number I include myself
Although sometimes I am doubtful
Mornings I awake full of stiffness
To look at the last stars
At the clouds gathering in the cold
And wonder
If there is more in store for me
Than these goats
These few sheep
But I am willing to go on as I am
Among the many ways men have devised to die while still on their feet
Goats at least are an honorable and harmless profession

## After Alberto Caeiro (4)

When will I die?
And does it matter
Is it even sensible
This question of when?
The goats do not think such things
They do not question, laugh, or cry
They have no need to do so
As I must
So it may be that goats do not die
Because to think of dying
Which is not possible to do
Except as a groping, urging one onward
In time

Is to die
And not to think
Of dying
To have no such word, no such thought, no such question
No such emotion or lack of emotion
Associated with such a thought or word
Is not to die, so goats do not die?
And if as it may be
My own thought of death
Is a self-reflexive impasse
A waiting room at the frontiers of thought
Full of benches and walls
Constructed from confusion
A reflex of the language I speak
A crude local dialect
And therefore not really a thought of death at all
But simply an expression of fear, my own fear
Or perhaps a fear I have received from the goats
Who have no other means of expressing fear
Save through me
Or is if not that then possibly my dialect itself
Expressing its locale and limit
Then it is possible I too do not die

## After Alberto Caeiro (5)

From this hilltop
I can see the sun
Setting to the west
Becoming a blazing red ball
That flattens and resolves into a thin red line
That enflames the clouds
Enrobing them in yellow

As my life is enrobed in goat
Summer evenings are peaceful
The goats are quiet
In the dying of the light
Darkness comforts them as it does me
And they do not much mind the cold
That still comes with the darkness
Since they do not know it as cold
But only live it as sensation
The only possible sensation
And not even known as that
They cannot therefore complain of the cold
It does not matter to them
And it is possible that the cold
Does not exist for them
Surely it does not
But for me the cold
That seeps
Into the corners of my soul
Even this time of year
Brings strong bitterness
For it makes me remember the winter cold
That I cannot let go of
That has become my chief thought
Accompanying all other thoughts
That come to mind
The defining feature of my life
Shape of my mood and temperament
Cause of the curses I fling upward to the sky
Against a God I seem not to believe in
Yet persistently blame
Even without naming Him
Or acknowledging Him
For the wound that is my life

This God
That in my resistance and despair
Lives more fully
Than He ever has
In prayers and observances
In the choirs of churches
In thinking
In sensation
In the emotion
Of being here among goats
Dumb undying aromatic stubborn goats
That will never go away
That do not die and do not know
They have been born
Here among the silences of spaces darkened and lit
And too seldom warmed
By the sun
That seems to want to go and return
Without cease and without ever once
Stopping its relentless movement
This God lives and quietly fails
To console
Other than in
Listening to these words
I have been speaking
It turns out to Him
Not to you, dear reader,
He Who unlike you
Does not mock
Or judge for good or ill
But only
Without sighing or bitterness
And without explicit response
But with a totality of covering absence

And equanimous clarity
Causes the words to echo
So that my heart hears them
And is comforted
More than a person could comfort
More than a goat

ooooo

## *from* Prayers

By Reb Yosl of Kemenetz, a simple tailor of Lithuania (circa 1820)

Prayer to Remove Fear and See the World's Beauty

Why is the wind so startling
When in autumn it stirs the grasses, drying out the plains
And so terrifying in winter when it whips the trees
Making me afraid the trees
Will uproot and fall upon my house, God forbid
Oh God!
You who aren't afraid of winds
Or trees or night
Or of me
Please grant
Though I am unworthy of your graciousness
(Given the meagerness of my acts
The weakness of my love
And the distraction I feel each day
In the prayer house when my mind wanders
To common unexalted thoughts)
That my heart be purified

Let my deeds and the words I utter from this day forth
Whip the roughness from my soul
To cleanse and polish my eyes
So that your world will shine in them
Startlingly and with fear of you

ooooo

## Prayer for my Wife

This is a prayer for my wife dear God
Who moves
No matter where she moves
Whether in air, on earth, or under water, God forbid
At the precise center of my life
(Where I know you should live, forgive me)
In the fullness of every good thought
Every worthwhile and kind deed I do
Oh God praise her and protect her so she won't
Get sick or be seriously hurt by anything
And since I know that because of my sins
And the weakness of the flesh so poor as always in your eyes
This is impossible
I am asking you to do it anyway because you are the God
Who turned back the seas, fed us in the wilderness, leading us by a pillar
    of fire
And such things for you are surely possible should you wish to grant them
Or, if you are offended by my asking
Please instead grant
That her falls not be from high places
And her scrapes and bruises not so rough and painful
And that the heavy pots she lifts, the pails of milk

Be made slightly less weighty in her arms
May her soul sufferings be likewise lightened
Lifted up gently toward heaven by your ministering angels
So that she will become used to them and not complain
And when dear God I am gone away and cannot help her
Please do your best to be her support
So that she be well and safe and happy and satisfied
In a world that is well enough and sufficient
And I bless you God in advance for granting these things
And for providing me with such a radiant bride

ooooo

## Prayer for Peace

O God I am wondering why people come to the point
Of feeling justified in their bitterness
So that the killing of one another
And of thousands even possibly millions of innocent victims
Makes sense to them and seems necessary
Some people say that if you God
Were actually in charge as much as Torah says you are
That this would never happen
That there would be peace in the land
The lion lying down with the lamb etc. as it is written
But we have never seen such things
Only have we seen the slaughter of our people
God forbid again and again
Which must mean either you are not in charge
Or are yourself the author of these atrocities
Or that we don't understand you
Yes I am sure that this is it, that we don't understand

And so my prayer for peace must be:
Help us God to understand your ways
Just enough
So that we stop ruining ourselves
So that our anguished weeping at war and human strife
Will cease at last, so that we, not you,
Will put violence aside
In a world of days and nights

ooooo

## Prayer for Laborers

May all who labor with their hands
Those who clean and cook, make beds and remove garbage
Those who fashion things of this world
As you have fashioned this world
Of words of your mouth
Those who make small things crafted by hand
Or very large things in the city's factories
But especially the smaller things of the earth
Made in small workshops near here
Things like shirts or spoons or shoes
Carts, pins and paper, buckets, rope
May all who make these things
Receive from you special blessings and extra protections
Because they are noble
And deserve the best of your care

ooooo

## Upheavals in Feeling

To refer to a life in poetry
I am living or leading
Somewhere under the carpet, in the quiet,
Or around the corner, beyond the pale
Upon which I remark, squeak about, or subtly weave
Is to make a mark on water,
Draw an edge for the sky

I know too much and not enough
My seat is warm

To think a pot holding water is partly full of water
Is to place three words at the cliff's edge
In order to see them fall slowly
Into the sea
Is nothing like the song I am seducing myself into
Through a life I suppose I am living or leading
At the edge of some sky

Rhyme is a blanket, meaning a train
Since no one has died time stands on its brain
Making hushed announcements
This is the rapture
My eyes so tired out
From this effort of looking
Into the edge of some sky

Exhausted in the invisible
Other voices play at other minds
Like a lyre or a loincloth devoid of its table
These dreary machinations skirt newness now

What is new?
Feeling.

I cast out my spinners and drifters
Their nets low and cut
Some fishes are sure to enter into their lapses
Despite feeling time's notions remain sequential
I only need a book and
To be close to a river
I do not even need to read the book
I remember every instance trapped in its net
I think I know
This pattern

Old dilemmas, feelings
Music of footfalls of breathing
The page would part and open like a wind
A gap in its whiteness frozen as snow
Sold solid and cold
Without a mark on it

Music like softballs large and imposing
A singular set of obsolete obsessions
Slower, as flowers
Solid as stones
A complete set of obsolete concerns and expressions
Commodious feelings sold solid as ice

Ice frames like dressers
The death of the author, the life of the form
The death of the form, the life of the culture
The death of a culture
Purging itself of the same obsessions, the old dilemmas

Moving the furniture around amid echoes
Like flowers in hallways
Long wide rooms hung with paintings
Dark paintings on dark walls (the known)
In a dark country at a dark time (the unknown)
Here though it is very bright by the sea
That sits minding its own business below a bright sky
I only have eyes for you

Pure of heart, simple of spirit
Collector of elaborate debris
Bring forth from within the outer airiness
Divesting without the inner dupes
Here is my list of ideas
Which I offer you as flowers

See how brightly red these poppies are
Turning and turning, long and long
On their fuzzy slender stems
Echoes of the smoking mountain
Pungent if unnoticed
The expense of losing everything
That ever happens to you
Whether or not you know

Here is my salsa, a city on fire
Or is it cloud I am seeing, not flame.
It is flame
In its frame, or fame of the artist or framer.
How do I know the tribes?

Why are these people huddled together
Murmuring and gesticulating?
Do they make me feel when

I do not know what they are saying
Or know and do not understand
Or think I understand and disagree.
A poem is a flower, a seashore, a pinecone-anemone
A gesture, a cliff, a hat brim, a pony —
This conversation cannot be a poem
Is language aghast and gone astray

(for Andres and Marisa Siegal)

ooooo

## *from* Versions of Saigyo

2.
How good it is
For the body to cry
Until it becomes a lake
Into which the heart
(A dark lump)
Pulls the moon down

8.
I dream my mother's face
As face of someone else, picture
In a foreign language newspaper . . .
Unhidden I have given up the world it's cheap
But have not known it, wear worldly clothes
A fool pretending to transcend time which pierces me

9.
I push through snow my face is snow
Entire snow white surf on Kiso's
Hanging bridge not a thing moves which is moving
A tool to open the danger
So deep I cannot see the bottom

24.
Stuck on the pivot of my knowing well what's perfect
    As jewel gleam on crest of wave can't be grasped
    As mind's light clear in glancing
Is neither so in me nor not so
    Which I suffer

26.
People who think Vulture Peak's moon
    Shakyamuni's set from before
To be dreamed of now or adhere to rule or letter
Are themselves dim all the way to dark

30.
Longed for guests
Who never arrived in ordinary presence to my mountain hut . . .

My disappointment equals glee in taste
Of happy loneliness
That brought me this

31.
When what's expected fails
    Or mind can't seize on what's to be

Expected grief rains down
Disorganized as cherry petals in this wind

ooooo

## After a Poem of Robert Creeley, Circulated Online After His Death

1.

When I think of my life, whatever life it is or has been,
of how time passes or seems to pass, when I recall days, weeks,
specifics, the river running by below me as I walked across one
of several bridges or the daily waking up, in rooms or under sky,
come back to gravity, identity, the physical world, sleeping,
speaking a plain language, thinking, imagining a future
that would never come, that was always & only now, here,
as this here, this now of remembering, writing, memory's fatal touch,
how strange it all is & always was — how hard I strained to grasp
even a grain of it, a straw of it, to somehow reproduce or produce
to match the sweep of it but never could, only ever unsatisfied in all
productions, that always fell, dissolved, but only in the process of their clumsy
making some fleeting sense of recognition, as if something for a moment
known or seen — & was I, I thought, the same person, or another,
a separate one or one of many nearly identical ones, never wanting to stand out or
apart, to be anyone, yet always straining upward or outward, forward,
toward the light I suppose, as dumb plant, the so-called future, imagined,
which is the past, so holding myself — I couldn't help it — apart for that
and at the end of all this I think it will come clear as dust motes or fog particles
burst bright upon the retina or the brain — pain — so living flares not as organized
story, but in chunks, moments, flashes of color, how lucky it was to be alive.

2.

Thinking of love, of loving you, simply that, but no the word
has too much been drained, its pungency, color, paled, so lets say I
appreciate that it has been for so long possible to care so much, so warmly,
& — miracle of all! — your intense touching care for me, its constancy,
that like food to the hungry (& not only basic sustenance but dishes proffered
with delicacy and abundance) has been given through all these days, these advanc-
ing years, who could have expected it, it must be that an animal passion, once yielded to,
guides our hands, our feet, in walking side by side, hand in hand, at a pace
through all the nights spent spooned together in the various beds, the many places
on earth, spots of warmth there because we were together there, blindly, dumbly,
& perfectly because dumbly blindly cleaved, like the sky, to each other, persons,
male and female of them, & the nights spent apart, each alone in darkness thinking of or not
thinking of but being half of what we otherwise were, one of us, us, out of which others
came as if it were a destiny to be so, as if it mattered or had specific meaning
that echoed through the worlds we made, that made us, in the households, meals,
the silent landscapes, sound of temple bells, the tears, the hurt, so much laughter,
so much shared and remembered through the flowing time & times, the history
of the billions of all of them small but always there in the life we've lived,
loved, yes somehow loved, the word now comes back to itself
through what we've weathered and made real, or seemed to make, guided to it
in dark ways we never imagined when we began.

ooooo

## *from* Seasons

in high spring
everything wants
to grow, strains
up haplessly —

days so long
evening keeps us
outdoors for light
calls

& nothing rests
even night's coolness
is a drawing up of
strength for next

day's yearning —
soft-mouthed new deer
have so much
to eat!

they walk trail or
cross road sur-
prised &
high-spirited

*

September
evokes
a place

in the mouth,
month of long
shadows

& sorrows
piled up bones
in an open field

in this month
I reckon
on things

that could be
said, could be
known as

rivers to snake
toward the
final sea

how not so
not so
it all is

this world-affirming
life-creating
stem

of a plant
on which cluster
tiny white

flowers
for the
season's end

—

not now
not then

not here
not there

*

so many days of fog
then not

can I even recall
winter's rains?

all the seasons
in a life

is it so very
long?

summer lasts
forever

its end ends
& where

does summer
move on to

what white
mysterious skies?

touching the tabletop
convinces

that it's there
eating seasonable plum

seems so
true to life

thanks to eye & sun
(eye that the sun
made)

I say I see
the Indonesian stool
blaze yellow light

they say that's
summer light,
the last

delicious
& apparent
rays

*

October

words a
stutter-
ing each

forced from
the
throat

drawn forth
pulled
out

through world's
sad
need

each a
pearl or
pool

bright with
cherished
promise

as if to fly
into the
face

of things
that call
for them

to complete
the
silence

even lit-
tle
pieces

of words
remnants
not of

thought or
feel-
ing

but for them-
selves,
words'

muse-
ic
their

utter
futile
charm

con-
tinu-
ous

human
necessity
skin &

flesh
air
they breathe

&
castles
they build

in
plain
air

*

what do you
or I or we
make of it,
anything

we do or
are in this
slant of
autumn's ancient

light?  I am
weary of the
harvest
I desired

all these ah-so-
fleshy apples
that still not
eaten

rot &
fade to
earth — there's
something

still on the edge
of being's candle
a
darkness

cannot come to
light but in
my
dream

lights all
the world
makes of autumn's
ripeness

a blaze
of color,
softness
of form

—

how the trees
as fuzz
yellow or red

flit by
auto's win-
dow

with a feeling
of the
past, winter's

coming? or
the death
I've been

expecting
so long
covered now

in snow or
crisp
clear air?

seasons make
the man
or wake him

to the sorry
state that is
himself

in passing yet
each one's
glorious estate

in tem-
porary beauty
exalts

the possible
demanding
imperative

that one's life's
witnessed — can
it be?

who knows
this or
otherwise

knows autumn's
secret
stirring

deep among
the fallen
leaves

*

the dead
know
nothing

& in this
provide
the widest

possible
wisdom, the
only

truth
in
town,

still (they
are so
still)

to ask
of them
help

is in a
way
futile

though no
help
other-

wise would
be
as true

*

"Someone else's business
is boldly attached to this
and there's no time

for a reckoning, the
carpet never stretches
quite far enough;

there's always
a footfall
on the stair"

# Conflict

2012

torture confronts

the painful truth

that each has its price

&

there are reasons

always reasons

laws

& rules

peacefully

point the way to pain

hills become lover ,

nemesis , kin

whoever wrote the memo remember what to protect

crack in the door — everything sucked out through the little opening the photos , humiliation

being one the pride of knowing one

what one proffers to be known

gone when you don't sleep

crushed when you can't breathe

out of control , in a panic

who takes satisfaction

where oblivion's the matter

to be wood

the body only bears so much

Akiva raked with combs

till his flesh tore off

climbed the final rung with "Hear!"

who pays the ultimate price

how can you sleep when you know ?

forgive the sinner , the powerful

make the strong weak

puncturing the soul , the will's

the flesh's weakness

when it depends on me

what & who I am

erect now

a golden calf :

worship ,

believe ,

absolutely believe

pain comes in waves

they do & don't relent

come in , go out

as long as life abides

in time , sensation

the heart detects its reasons

how much I depend

on standing up , breathing air , moving in time , space

limbs & sinews at rest

without pressure

how easily the world dissolves absent this accustomed ease

an animal merely knows no horror outside its life

what's worth protecting

to what extent

&

when

does protection

exceed that worth

its cost in pain

overreaching

the value of existing

which always had

a not in it ,

a knot , is there something

I should be dying for ? Can I choose it ?

no , it is not right

therefore

I must kill you

or if not

gouge out a hole

in what you love

&

hold more dear

than life — demeaning

that , a world dissolves in smoke , rising

what's truly unbearable?

we bear
what we bear

&

go

shouting is not raping

raping is not stabbing

stabbing is not shooting dead

dismembering , beheading , gouging out

the eyes , skinning alive

burning at the stake

for your actions of the past

for what you

profess

for your kinship , your place of residence

your skin , your words , your possessions

for what I see as myself

my size — my meaning

I protect

follow the thread

of my passion my will

"there's no forgetting this

ever"

fool myself with my argument

only to live and go on living

in its face

motivated

the rest comes behind ,

pelicans following a boat

naked statements of fact

do not move me they are not so

I do not see

my

enemy

passion , not human

his reasons are crimes

to make the world a nightmare

I have dreamed

to prevent which I sleep screaming

a nightmare I don't know I live

a world of limited possibilities

all artifice &

smear

cutting off the simple

music

for tortured silence

no statement possible

I know too much to speak

well , what used to be funny

still is , falling down

when you least expect it pushing a stone uphill

your beauty's source

a question

removed without reply

, the world ,

poured into

the dark opening

that you are

&	not

not given	,

made

— & the difference ? —

thus unstable

pursuing itself ,

clawing

your second nature	,	culture	,	the totality of human products

the earth throws off	like wind

sadly smoky	glazed with your absence

Lahore	,	dozens

trapped in the rubble

two arrested	—	men

get out of the car shooting

hundreds to hospital

"I was there on duty

. . . . . the gunfire continued

. . . .. the building collapsed"

at any time

can destroy our lives

or anyone

anywhere

which is ever the case

"Any hostile act

Upon our borders

Will be considered

An act of war"

Short range missiles

The treaty is done ,

She shouts

With a power behind her person

Welcome to you both

For the ominous

Challenge you face

break out or bust out

states go nuclear quickly

we must cool the situation

which is unprecedented

lest they fall into the hands .....

an immediate task

the hope & expectation

("we always say

those sorts of things")

good faith try

how we defend ourselves

containing . . . . .  limiting . . . . .

ratchet up , ratchet down

a new action for instance North Korea , Libya , Syria ,
China , Russia , Japan —

Painful & visible
At risk , alone

ooooo

Instructed by God

Both sons of Abraham

Christians , Muslims

This dusty Lagos neighborhood

Torn apart or cleared

All are Christian

The lame are walking

And the blind are now seeing

"*Why have I not*

*found favor in your eyes*

*to set the burden*

*of this entire people*

*on              me              now*

*Did I conceive this  ?*

*Birth it  ?*

*That you should tell me*

*'Carry them all the way home*

*as father , mother ,*

*And they cry at me , 'Give*

*us meat*

*to eat , give us meat!' Well*

*Kill me! Kill me if that is*

*How it is"*

Humans and their Maker

have an undying basis

of conflict

the one beyond

the other inside

the one inside

the other beyond

Imperfect speech

Strains

to divide   ,   unite

as they are as

they are not

Eve   . . . . .   Cain   . . . . .   Moses   . . . . .

The divine   /   human   tangle

the head  ,  the voice  ,  saw daily   the wonders

yet moan   ,   murder   ,   maraud

*"And the relations*

*between God*

*and Abraham's descendants*

*are aimed*

*eventually*

*at resolving*

*this"*

damage. . . .

the whole of it lost it seems at sea. . . .

no mere dis-

integration, a jewel-like collapse ,

sea-change

in the soul

devolving distractions

all a fever to the foam

Now

more

speak — you — too

# The Strugglers

2013

## *from* Sixty-Five

1. I can't walk across the room without forgetting why I wanted to do that, what I was after. I arrive at the other end of the room, I don't know why I am there, I can't tell in what precise sense I am there, is it some sort of trick, an illusion?

2. I am upstairs, I don't know why. Finding myself at this new level, I wonder whether I ought to be here, whether I actually am here, whether it actually is another level in relation to the previous level, or whether my sense of having changed levels is accurate, since I seem to have been on this level continuously.

3. Sometimes I recover my purpose by stopping. I leave a space for thinking. Something occurs to me, something new. It is not my original purpose. So I have new purposes.

4. I am caught in the daily, physical, specific, detail of my life. But I can't tell what this means to me. To what extent is all this a theory, fruit of contemplation, artifact of language, training — the chair, the table, the refrigerator, the pencil, the impulse to wipe the counter.

5. I made a video of that, I sent a link. It went everywhere, all over the world, though not to anyone specifically. So far no one has responded. Maybe they could not open the link. That happens. Maybe the video was devoid of images. Maybe it had duration, it began, it ended, but no images.

6. Nothing is repeated. Each moment is new. When you are here you are here. When you are gone you are gone. Does that count? Does absence occupy time, is absence a new moment? Does it have its own sort of presence? How intelligent the aggressive others, who live in great cities, who write books. Who know facts. Have opinions that matter to others who have opinions that matter to others. Tonight I saw moonlight on the patio. I saw blooming plum trees like white clouds against the grim background of darkened buildings.

7. The computer screen's depth. Switched on, it glows, cool and detached. The underlying binary structure of everything. Formless and void, and then : let there be light! Words dividing the chaos. Life, death, so simple, so clear. Or is it just confusion, wishful thinking, finger in the dike?

8. Thirty to forty minutes and it's done. Then I can begin. Travel is broadening. Your life story, a frame around a picture, a basic mood or thrust. Blink your eyes and . . . a life gone by. Just like that, as they say. The flowers are breathing too, in the same rhythm.

9. It's so difficult to come up with something. Nine gateways to the body, guarding inside from outside. Yet you always take things in, give them out. There's no purity. There's no integrity.

10. The gangly rosebushes bristling in the wind. It couldn't be any more austere than that. How you put a world together, by will and idea. Until you can cut it with a knife.

. . .

20. It follows that existence — being here as a function of doing, perceiving, giving, receiving, communicating — comes to a sort of dither. It is neither here nor there. People talk to the dead all the time. The dead have the best information.

21. The rabbis don't argue about this, because they are duty bound to be certain about something. The rules are not made up. As I spread my arms wide I sigh, I weep, releasing a host of assumptions. Life turns on its head. I make culture, I know how to do things. I have memory, I respect the past. I follow the rules, I am the one who is alive. I will not be undone with too much doubt.

22. When I come downstairs a telephone is ringing. An intruder on my pure subjectivity. How can I know myself if I don't know the one at the end of the line? Experience is alienating. Misleading. Being a person always is. It constellates another. And in another's absence, the revision is in the beginning, always was. The past darkens. The grass illuminates. A beginning includes an ending. Why God must be my good friend.

23. So I came here to let something fall from my grip. It's in the drawer, a world I can improve. Passion's twist, my childhood, my parents. Here they are. We danced. We never sat down. We coaxed the wallflowers into dancing too. I'm here on the couch, water dripping from the eaves. I'm a person, beyond artifice, beyond genre. I am my own genre, template, limitation, what I say is what needs to be.

24. Orchids in a vase, ceramic dishes. Underwater invertebrates, surpassing strange. Little whirring fins, a delicate locomotion. All genres express love. All love exfoliates death. People kill as an improvement technique? Is that what this has been about? Whatever needs to be is, by being that, all forms end at their edges. So I keep on listening to the tale. At the wall — the wall.

25. The urge toward dominance, or more of the same, is a feature of language. Held in comforting arms.

. . .

34. Persistent dream of an idealized past or perfect future. The wisdom of crowds — the sum of our lunacy yields the best results. Bad results. Numbers always add up to zero. Hope and nostalgia are functions of language, thought is hopeful and wistful, to tie two twigs together with soap. I think the green hills, they think me. Who know whether they are there, depending on my being here. Hardness, softness, color and shape.  A currency of ideas. We can't all be crazy in the same way or at the same time.

35. A symbolic system engages me with the ultimate conditions of my existence. A set of notes, metaphors, rituals and rules. I used to like it but now I don't. I used to be one but now I am many. I used to be you but now I am me. Then I fell when the sun melted my wings. Plunged into the sea. And the farmer wiped his brow, the dray horses plowed on, the little girl drank cream and brushed her hair away from her eyes. The world rolled on.

36. The need to know — or at least imagine. How have dealings with you if I don't know who you are and who I am and what we are dealing in. It seems to be insufficient simply to get though the day. Does utilitarian individualism free us from bondage? Which is what, to what? Finishing the hat. How does the smoking mountain play out its drama if not through force of sound, melody of demanding words. Do this, don't do that. Is love the drama implied in wine and bread, lilies of the field? Lay down the law — in both senses. Sigh and move on or fight and gasp till you drop. It comes at the end of an era that the one you love is cancelled. The feeling of losing everything is worse than it seems. Even the landscape weeps for want of mcaning. It needs a reason to bloom.

. . .

61. A pressure as the wall's approached. It's in illumined grasses, you sense an aura around your words. I'm not sure how I knew. But what a surprise. Dreamed before or later. Not words exactly, not pictures or sounds, but senses of things that the named perceived thing would only dimly suggest, the things and their presences, not physical but not not. All of this is your body. Now that the wall's dissolved. And the orchard behind it. We do not have any words for that. Our words only take us this far. Here we set them gently down in the grass. But going this far we are already where we must be. We use words to say that.

62. Becoming still more unspeakable. Can't defend any action, all action brings dire result. Everything ends badly because it ends at all. The prayer shawl that wrapped you. The illumined presence, not a face anyone could see, yet we called it a face, and we said, you cannot see the face, and did not know what we meant though we were certain when we said it. The contradictions confirm themselves, connected as they are to their absences, which are yours.

63. The rabbis spoke of God as if they knew him, they did. In sacred syllables events going on there, praising each other, speaking in each other's name, no one can, it's in the praise itself, wailing at the wall, waiting for generations there, nothing happens — and brings violence.

64. Of endings, none. Of stopping, nothing. Of evening and of morning, one day. Then seven. Then twelve. Then more. Explosions of being, which is affluent. One which is dark.

65. Not wanting to say good-bye. God be with you, you be with God in sky, cloud, field. Not wanting to hear dirt drum on pine casket, decisive, mournful, distinct, shoveling till hole's filled up, and you are tucked in earth asleep. Why insist on one? What is one? In the things that fly up and over, so many, the days the weeks the years. The secret endings begin again, what place there is seems glum, I set my jaw, am Jew, am word, and tested.

*(for Alan Lew November 10, 1943 - January 12, 2009, in his memory)*

ooooo

## *from* The Strugglers

### Their Claws

The strugglers with their claws reach in but are snatched by — or they snatch —
From the streaming crowds of superannuated people in blistering cold with their
 nystagmic impulses
Aggressive and violent, darkly arrayed among the streets and towers destruct and
 self-destruct blindly
Without words for this, concepts or knowledge, impressions, images, to reach with
 such red claws
All innocent, brutally dumb, they extract hearts, blue hearts
What do they want them for? What do they do with them?

ooooo

### Wearing Coats

The girls in their frocks across the crowds or in them
As a parade, a wave, the crowd not as blood in blood vessels exposing parts to wholes
But alone standing in their midst as victims of them the red claws reaching into them
The girls' plumes as their blue hearts where the violent man reaching into
The lining of the stomach eroded already by acidic/corrosive emotion
Action to swirl or choke, thrust down, burbling up the girls bursting out of that
In a pink blossom to extract blue hearts from them

ooooo

## Not The Case

The only thing that's real's the grief one writes of what's the case
Even if not [the not no words in]
In the imagination had to figure out what's played out nice fish pieces carefully arranged
Photos of that taken at any earlier time what's lined up sensibly to be the world
Of Events, People, Place, like mercury adhering then not that would be any religion
that says,
THIS IS HAPPENING AND THEN NOT so as they say you are dead it's the
end of the story
And what about the one
Who actually is dead
Not now writing this
Or
Later
As you read
Having been dead now having written
As always inspired by grief
The general grief
Of the one who's living not yet having died while others die, always others
Or the writing as the creation of that, words as memorials inevitable
What about this that can be said, that's felt
What about that way of putting it's not the case

ooooo

## Rushing Through Factories

As if in a panic when the election was rigged
As the Han rushed through Uighers' factories killing them
As if in a panic, a frenzied agitation, as a tick, as if having to decide suddenly
Whether to kill or be killed these actions not events outside

But inside — the pressure of their feeling — as if outside
Had burst in in the mobs rushing through factories
Leaving the orphan girls as slaves almost from birth, to be prostitutes for them because of their terror
Seemingly urgently needing some kind of violence in sex that themselves they'd never do but because of the terror & panic
Do do flashing messages to one another to gather in the square to protest non-violently but the government
With superior force of arms as if protecting each person from the emotion inside that person
Or fear or terror of what could happen monstrously imagined when things are completely out of control
Smashing their heads open — is thrilling — to see their glistening blood is calming them the next day

ooooo

## Swinging Spacious Determinators

Then the stream rushing by is young girls it's not water
Rushing by with history's full force everything's so dysfunctional
Violence is normal, violation's normal, this is what
They make TV shows about because it's the water we drink therefore
Of the passion the girls become water not people yet not yet that
Because of the trauma that's common as water, as dirt
They wear dog-tags they commune with dogs who are kind to them
Understand them, growing on trees, pulling the fruit from trees
As if monkeys but they're lost in the branches
Can't see, can't feel earth beneath their feet, they're nowhere
They swing from branch to branch implicitly fearing a fall
That will end their servitude as a cake-walk
Without mercy, the words mercy, repentance, forgiveness, sin

Having no longer any meaning, nor violence, violation, servitude
As far as the skateboarders are concerned there's no sense at all
Beyond speed and the need to ride up walls defying gravity

ooooo

## Oceans in Arab Spring

When they took to the streets due to Twitter-feeds
Facebook posts the square crowded with cattle-people, their ribbons
Painted as floats in a parade bright green leaves, plumes
Subject to perspectives of the onlookers who see only the insides of their own veins,
the impulses
Twitter-feed servers being carnival-like what matters injurious to their rising
When the men on horses and camels (as with the young girls perpetual slaves)
To their fathers in cabinets like street stars seen on CNN looking for a savior
Having consulted experts saying that they do not understand but that they are moved
to tears
All having seen in diarthria utter disregard cantankerous as to future prospects
Fray of dispirited baserunners foggy dysphemia
As if a green perfect world is possibly contained there (within the confines of the park
with its rules)
Where events elsewhere seen only by others
But not as for floating through those most involved as close to one
But from books? As events replacing times in time's muddles?
In the probably bloodstream larger as metonymy for as large and the very small

ooooo

# What's Found Underneath That

Whole smarmy floral dichronics
Where there's an opening into cavities where they say beauty lies [but they lie]
Torque inside the hole, bulbous, seen from outside, so the one outside
Is the possessor, possesses the inside as the object of the outside, in relation to it,
One's self seen as inside the flower with its cavity in which they lie, about it,
Hole or bowl, the bawcock remains glad slaps the backs of the backers
Who supply the corporate money, friends to get things done, hearts in the right place,
You must play ball, they say, play the game to get things done, can't sit out, no good
To be idealist, cleave ideal, eternal, essence, she's to be Romantic not that or this
Yet the deb amid the rubble found there a nose/finger what's
Smashed beneath plaster and steel, Saito, as the wave rises up the boatman seeing it
[He thinking the island would not have transport that without food
They'd die, stranded, would need assistance, no one would come, motivated by this
Turned the boat toward the wave against the impulse to turn away, released to it]
So sped boat into wave taller than tall Tokyo building, solid water wall, rose atop it
Through and over, saved boat and island though nearly everyone had died as they
Pieced through rubble to find photos, keepsakes, bodies, memories, to prove
They'd been there historical time's not now as eternity so the prescient abducent moment
As transfection into the present as one's writing, the ordinary's
Not so ordinary as it seems, smeared with conceptators' blood,
To make it strange isn't — it's already that, stained with it,
This/that as one mountain here and another there, one moves from one
Is the other simultaneous, they are simultaneous, the deb remembered tore down the dress
They kissed twice on the terrace she in white in the Cathedral they pierced by stars that fell
(If and when they fell into another day, stars, everything would be over suddenly then all
Cultural production's cavity, a spur, a spire, stalled in memory but no one's memory, record
Notations holding sounds requiring sensible ears

ooooo

## Imagined at a Distance

The lost orphan/child in rubble is never so bad as imagined from Boston, from
image [it is
Not image because not contextualized] the earthquake seemed so much worse in
Boston, James said,
Though there were fires in buildings, streets smashed, rubble, debris, corpses, but
that Was merely Present, surrounding scene becoming ordinary the
difference between being and not
That you saw cadavers was ordinary, corpse is ordinary/flesh mundane
So a hollow concavity is dawn the tanks' shooting of Qadaffi that took the city
Hemmed it in then not as drone took out tanks become adductions of
rubble, chemical
Rebels ran shooting aimlessly as xylum through time's sense in language
Flowing through as yesterday flows to them as food for today
That events happen one at a time in separate places/not so/also so/as existing
Then as if such could be the case there, that the PEOPLE say so
But no way to find out what PEOPLE
In Twitter-feed nightmare they don't say what they feel they don't exist there
In tranquility they excited feel taking on Twitter personna
For there's no inside they can find they find only outside as soon as
Inside's seen or known it's outside something to clutch
So self-aggression, mutilation, suicide, despair's inevitable condition of speech/soul

ooooo

## Water Walls

Because the immense wall of water coming ever closer gathering speed and
mass
The Morganza spillway's set to open to release water (1.5 million cubic feet
per second)

Into Mississippi delta, Operation Watershed social media New York Times
says on Huff Post
THANK EACH OF YOU FOR YOUR COLLECTIVE WORK FOR
OUR SAFETY GOD BLESS
As the planes strafe Qadaffi's palace men flee women say "they are weak
they don't live here anymore"
So she attacks the dor, is attacked by it (it's "beetle" and "mocking" both,
she's marked by the water it dwarfs her)
Several lexemes stuffed or strafed with the planes, this might be a stalemate
prolonged civil war
But she takes the authority she sets all the notes and rules then violates them
D O N'T G O N E A R A W O M A N as the mountain smokes it blows
600,00 people back 12 miles
Whose souls separate from bodies as horns blare, it's baggage, choreutic, in
T O T A L S I L E N C E
Which even the angels specializing in singing HOLy,HOLy,HOLy cease
from this their lips sealed
Paying such close attention to her time going back forward and back
(meaning time's not going, not flowing, not like the water)
It ends up somewhere, its power spread, time going/not going at the speed
of graduated minutes/frames per second produces
The illusion of smoothness, it's not smooth one's no idea what goes on here
Design's unintelligent, system's senseless, logic-resistant [no thought of
that] out in umiak woman's boat
Ice floes maybe reindeer or elk, maybe moose, Sarah Palin shoots
Killing with one shot health care system record profits for medical
insurance companies
Oil companies they do it just for you, there's lenticular discourse here
Peened, daily peened, pocked with small pellets daily softens one for the kill

ooooo

## Sanctus

"Sanctus. Sanctus. Sanctus." That there could be experience, brain-sites, memory, that past is now
The dead alive
Is certainly not that that's so that being says it's so is so as a saying in time
That's fictional [absence being presence] but put together fictionally construes a world to shout out at
So peacefully, a lake in which trees reversed seen as reflection one reflecting another, trees, moon sliver
That therefore nothing occurs, has, will, is, was occurring, that these
As time's shape in the lips conditions it, sinks into, depth requires surface
Sites in brain flashpoints there as incertitude, indeterminacy, whirring machines, no erasure, numbers real
They cite their refusals, resistances, there's red light sacrum pain blindings, pain flooding brain-sites
Wanting to know one knows nothing ever pressing onward toward a further knowing
One is one, already by that cognition two, if two infinite more
Literally no end or boundary, anyway expanding outward into more nothing/something

ooooo

## Interior Insects

Thence into emerald dark ballplayers whacking rubber ball against sloped ascending stone court
Sweating bare-chested in heat recalling imagistic materialistic earth's lying flat in dark
Adam Smith's knowing the moral sense keeps people in check assuming there's connection to what's done
That numbers don't spin out of control parsed endless tricked by flesh or they

trick flesh
No one yet knows rules of that game but it's known that the losers must die,
sacrificed to gods
Later high up on temple pavilions (very small altars large enough only for single
priest that high up)
Priests pierce penis with pointed awl must bleed from there as gods require this
They'd suffered myxedema so not knowing the effects of their acts
All smothered in general mysophobia so covering all with plastic or tin foil, aptrous
They fall, dystrophy of the ball players now so all must die
(They play as surrogates for population somehow in their dysuria painful pissing
yellow stream in annulated dribblings
Insects rose up as if born from the urine swarming the audile rhizocarpous micturations
prodigious blastosporic fluctuations that [in one's nightmare that's
Now occurring] universally encoats the planet erasing all color, all distinct shape so
that all's wriggling
Horrific movement of tiny wings, feet, furious appetites devour as moving en masse
cancrine)
In a present swallowing the past, no room for grief or even feeling in the fury of it,
there's no feeling,
All time squirming in a pullulating present overwhelming the sensations,
there's no thought

ooooo

## Not in Chains

Such news as is seams or joints, studs, struts, held in frenulum
Most precious materials [he said, is saying] used in connectors, where con-
nected, for portability, no establishment, the rest's cheap, easily
replaced
The girls then running & hard to say whether toward or away {depending
on where one is standing as saying this}

A seam there, the present being outside yet the one seems [seams] to be
    inside time as if substance
Then linked to that, a dolmen, austere structure one's born inside & outside of
To lustrate occurrence, that it can be done, parachuting through time, a
    catenulation
Then the girl and white Alaska dog (fluffed as if a jetting ball) [both being
    pure & having perfect white teeth, the girl, innocent, to grin, dog
    to gnaw] running there on beach in fog
Pain-free then in robust air also's inside if so

*[for (fore) & after Leslie Scalapino's The Diehedrons Gazelle-Diehedrals Zoom, and in her memory]*

ooooo

## *from* Mandelstam/Stone or the Russian Mall Poems

. . .

My body — what to make of it
This thing my own, my personal gift

Who thank
For this joy of breath, of life?

I'm the gardener and the flower
Never alone in life's prison

My warmth, my breath, already
Etched on eternity's clear pane

Distinctive pattern now engrained
Known by no one's brain

And when my life's all drained
This pattern's shape remains
(8)

What's the use of speech?
What is there to teach?
How sorry the one-joke soul
How lonely, brutal, and sad

It has nothing it can teach
It lacks the power of speech
It dips like a dolphin, deeply swims
Subject to its accursed whims
(11)

. . .

It's freezing in here!
I can't feel anything!
But the sky's bright
And insists I yap —

Yearn, you idiot!
Be sentimental and tender
And catch the cold
The cosmos has entailed in you

Here's the poem
That links you to a world of hurt
That, sneezing and wheezing,
Cuts you finally down to size

Suppose from its cold mall on high
Where it offers daily specials and holiday discounts
A star should shoot down like a piercing cleaver
To slice apart your heart suddenly
(28)

. . .

It's not the moon it's my glowing iphone
That awakens me in the middle of the night
Don't blame me
If all my light is here below

I hate Botyushkhov's arrogance!
There's no eternity
Just minutes and hours between meals
And periods of lying down and rising up
(31)

. . .

A Lutheran

Past the mall a funeral comes
Procession of dark cars, silent, tall

A Lutheran has died
And though my thoughts were far away I saw
The parishioners were troubled, one and all

For death speaks a foreign tongue
The shoppers do not comprehend
Its silent words ring like a temple bell
Heard only by the very weary

The mourners look quite healthy
In J. Jill sheaths, Men's Warehouse suits,
Plunge into black cars somberly linked
Snaking up the freeway ramp

Hypocrite sadness, limo curtains close
A Lutheran to be buried
Prayers, tears, a rose

Whoever you were late Lutheran
You certainly have an impressive cortege
Everyone decorous, serious, they'll speak well of you
It's almost worth the oblivion

Your reputation encloses you
And this is what you have
The mall's digested everything else
As we return to our urgent pursuits
Like candles burning useless at midday
(37)

Passers-by speak of nothing
They cannot bear a dignified silence

So carry on in exaggerated concern
For prices, friends, current events

An invisible man standing to one side
Begins to speak in tones so strange
And words so obscure, shoppers, astounded,
Stop, stare, tremble, recompose, move haltingly on

For what else can be done
When words' meanings are crushed by the tongue,
Syntax, suddenly, in the hands of angels

Is he a Homer, a Heidegger, a saint or demon?
He stops, drinks water, returns to himself, stands dumb —
I pass this scene unnoticed
My shopping bags shaking in trembling hands
(40)

. . .

An American Girl

An American girl, age 30,
She wants to go to Egypt, Croatia, New York
She's beautiful, arrogant, undaunted
Wants to marry but loves her work

She would like to have children
She wants them soon
Currently purchasing a MacBook Air
She's bound for Paris, or the moon

Where in the Louvre's Pei's Pyramid
She stands illumined, fair as a poplar
She's an early adopter
Pinnacle of the Hominid
(52)

Dombey and Son

Dombey sat in the corner
In the armchair by the bed
Son lay in a basket warmer
His head like a muffin near the fire

Dombey was rather bald and red
Son was very bald and very red
Somewhat crushed and spotty
In his general effect, as yet

Time and Care had set their marks
On Dombey's brow, while Son's was crossed
With a thousand changeable creases
Which that same deceitful Time would soon emboss

Dombey, exultant, jiggled his gold watchchain
That depended from his trim blue coat
Son, with little fists curled and strained,
Punched at existence or made for its throat

The earth's arrayed
For Dombey and Son to trade in
The sun and moon
To offer them commercial light

Rivers and seas to float their ships
Rainbows to mellow their enterprising hearts
Winds blow favorably to their business
Stars and planets offer amortizing context
(53)

No victory and no war!
O Founding Fathers, how long must we serve
We who are condemned
To preserve the mall

From the Terror that forever lurks
On the nearside of the disembodied other
Ideationally re-worked
With bits of string and dumpster refuse

Rome was not built in a day!
But must it be rebuilt each day
In the locked and crowded precincts
Of our attenuated ever-purchasing hearts?
(57)

No grass grows on the moon
Not even a single blade
All the people on the moon
Are in the footwear trade

At my place on the moon
There are waffles every day
Come with me my darling Empress
Where we eat this way

Lets escape for an hour
From this overdone prison of earth
There aren't any malls on the moon
Only benches everywhere

When you step it's a leap
Across three benches!
Bring your kitties, rope,
And some strawberry jam,

An umbrella and a comb
I'll make you hot punch, Empress
On the moon
Where it's always twilight under the dome
(58)

...

Values are eternal, they'll always stand
Above the dull mistakes of the times
That scorned, because they didn't understand,
A poet who made his verse sublime

Poor Sumarokov whose plays express his misery
Who did not know of Banana Republic or Gap
Who buried himself in luxuriant solemnity
Not knowing it for what it was, a trap

Inwardly leaning, what can ever be done
To meet the soul's essentially outward thrust
No contemplative's a hero
Every mood and feeling brings mistrust
(64)

Nature is the same as Rome and mirrored there —
We see this also in REI's displays and programs
That set the tone for what we feel and see in lakes and canyons
That reflect the national epitome

Self, nature, mall, and nation
Together trumpet a clarion call
Read the entrails, wait at the station
Embark enslaved, enthralled
(65)

Let brief nations
Enjoy their day of chattering fame
It's not Rome that survives the centuries
But human mind's disdain

Presidents tap into it, priests aspire,
Product developers know it furthest
When they tune their hearts to desire —
Mall's its monument
(66)

. . .

And on Mount Athos even now
A tree miraculously springs
On the mountain's steep green brow
Where monks still sing

They rejoice in their lonely cells
Veneratora of God's name
Gospel's total joy to them
It heals their pain

But here in the mall
The monks can't bear the light
They twitch confused and dazzled
Withdraw in fright

For love's the great heresy
Crossing out both man and God
Love the mall and love the sinner
Love the store, the church, the quod
(75)

ooooo

## *from* A Young Girl, a Hierophant

. . .

Lets take for instance something in the room right now
That could be named and evoked
Pictured in the reader's mind's eye
Anything lurking in wait, that has heft
Sudden burst of pattern: and the bolt from the blue
Dispersed as soon as it gathers
Why can't I get what you're telling me?
What drag holds the corners tight?

In search of my emotional honesty
Lecturing into myself such force from behind
That tethered them, light years beyond it
But who decenters abstruse perceptionality
Into smoked decanters, that, as if coherent or denied
These feathers flutter between us
Why always the partition of the unsaid
As if they could express anything by their shouting
Equal to their murmuring squeals

I'm not pierced, it could be that
There's no other but in here
Wagered for the brunt of simulacrums
Waterlogged if pettifogging, and then frost
There are no more ideas out there
Wall's opaque to direct sunlight
Lilliputian orthodoxies sagging round
Crying out for my mothers, and then some

Floating, that what's seem's awry
Can I grasp anything, as if I were a person again
It's not that that's that or if this,
This and that, its that's me, or she

Flipping through pages rapidly — not that
But digits or feathers, but firm, flexible enough to rise and fall
Behind, then gone, succeeded by successors
The long ebb and flow of living beings replaying one another

Flesh reorganized in linear fashion through time
That flows by as sticky substance unidirectionally
As measured by clocks. Death would be a jokey metaphor.
The counting voice murmuring on

ooooo

## *from* Recognition

So many people to worry about, we can never come to the end of worrying about people/

So many people worrying about people, we can never come to the end of people worrying about people worrying about people/

So many worried people, we worry about them, we do not come to the end of worrying about them, we worry, they worry, we worry about them, they worry about us, they worry, we worry, we do not come to the end of this/

They worry, we worry, we worry about them, people people people people, they are not abstract, they do not come to an end, they come to an end, they come to the end, they come to their end, they come to our end, they never come to the end of worrying about them, we never come to the end of worrying about them when they are ending and coming to the end of their ending/

So many endings, so many people, people people people people, such worry of them, such worry about them, they worry, we worry, they never come to the end we worry about them ever there is never an end to our worry about people worrying about people/

So many people to worry about us, such we, such us, such them, such worry, such people, so many people, each one being one, each one being them, each another, each other and none other than her, me, I, then they, we, us, then them and we, such people, such worry, so many worries we can worry about, these those our their people people people people, there's never any end to it/

We worry about them, ever, never, forever, they, we, such worry about them is not abstract, they are facing us we see their faces and worry about them, there's no end to worrying about their faces facing our faces, facing them we worry about them facing us they worry about us, us and we and them and they and us and them worrying about their faces facing them their faces facing us worrying about us facing them/

There's no end to faces, no end to facing faces, faces facing faces, being a face, being faces, worrying about faces in consequence of that, to face being face, being face to face a face, being faces facing faces, it's worry, ever worry, never worry, with no end to it, how could there be an end to it/

We worry about their faces that are not abstract, living faces facing faces, living facing the faces in the living aliveness, expressions, animations, fluid, fragmented, fictive, fulminating, dancing faces, faces fanning out amid faces, thick-skinned faces, thin-skinned faces, dark faces, light faces, light and dark faces, faces of darkness, faces of light, forever faces, ever faces, never faces, we worry about them they are worried about us it's not abstract/

It's not abstract we worry about them forever going on worrying about them how could there be an end to this worry about the faces of them, worry about the faces of us or the faces of our or their or the faces of it or the faces of now and then their faces worrying about faces facing faces worried about them, their faces, hands, their feet, their worry, their feelings, their concerned faces facing concerned faces animated with worry for their faces facing them worried and concerned/

We worry about them, we never stop worrying about them, we worry, they worry, they go on, we go on, they fall and get up, they get up and fall again, we worry, we fall and get up, we get up and fall again, they fall, we fall, they get up, we get up, we fall together, we fall separately, we fall we get up, they fall they get up, this goes on it doesn't end/

## Acknowledgments

I have many people to thank for the production of this volume, representing thirty-three years and more of work in poetry. First, Denise Newman and Monica Heredia, who made the selections. I would not have known how to go about this. Next, Charles Alexander, of Chax, the publisher of the present volume, who has done so much to support innovative poetry over many decades, and has long been a personal friend, and a friend of my work. And to the many other editors of poetry presses and magazines, who have published me — too numerous to mention, but let me start with the late Gil Ott and Paul Naylor of Singing Horse Press, the late Leslie Scalapino of O Books, the late Peter Ganick of Potes and Poets Press, Susan Schultz of Tinfish Press, Ed Foster of Talisman House, Christophe Lamiot Enos, of Presse Universitaires du Rouen et Havre, Geoff Young of The Figures, and Sue Moon of Open Books, which issued my first full book. There are so many poets with whom I have been in dialog over these many years, whose encouragement, conversation and work has informed and inspired my own, poets of my own generation, poets of previous and succeeding generations. My deep gratitude and respect to you all.

## About the Author

Norman Fischer has published twenty-one books of poetry and six books on Buddhism. His poetry has been anthologized in *The Wisdom Anthology of North American Poetry, Basta Azzez enough, What Book*? and many literary magazines. He holds an MFA from the University of Iowa Writer's Workshop and a Masters in Buddhism from the Graduate Theological Union at the University of California at Berkeley. He has been a Zen Buddhist priest for more than 40 years, serving as co-abbot for the San Francisco Zen Center from 1995-2000. Founder and teacher of the Everyday Zen Foundation, he is one of the most highly respected Zen teachers in America, regularly leading Zen Buddhist retreats and events around the world. His essays have appeared in such notable collections as *Radical Poetics and Secular Jewish Culture* (University of Alabama Press, 2010) and are frequently included in *Best Buddhist Writing* (Shambhala). His collections of essays on writing, *Experience: Thinking, Writing, Language and Religion* (University of Alabama Press) and on Buddhism, *When You Greet Me I Bow* (Shambhala) are widely read, as is his translation of the Hebrew psalms, *Opening to You.*

## About Chax

Founded in 1984 in Tucson, Arizona, Chax has published more than 240 books in a variety of formats, including hand printed letterpress books and chapbooks, hybrid chapbooks, book arts editions, and trade paperback editions such as the book you are holding. From August 2014 until July 2018 Chax Press resided in Houston-Victoria Center for the Arts. Chax is a nonprofit 501(c)(3) organization which depends on suppport from various government & private funders, and, primarly, from individual donors and readers. In July 2018 Chax Press returned to Tucson.

Our current address is 1517 North Wilmot Road no. 264, Tucson, AZ 85712-4410.

You can email us at *chaxpress@chax.org.*

Your support of our projects as a reader, and as a benefactor, is much appreciated.

You may find CHAX at https://chax.org

Text & Display: Adobe Caslon Pro

Cover & Book Design: David Weiss

Cover photo: Norman Fischer

Printer & Binder: McNaughton & Gunn

Book design & production directed by Charles Alexander